THE WORKBOOK

Write Better at Work: The Workbook

The Author: Joseph Judge

Joe admits that he spent far too much time in school. It was while he was in college, majoring in engineering and in business, that he began to develop his passion for writing clearly. Beginning in the late 1970s, Joe was in and out of engineering school. His early career moves included: power plant construction for Westinghouse, power systems design for Exxon refineries, and government aircraft proposals for Lockheed. In between these assignments, he earned 3 masters degrees in engineering from Rensselaer. After this Joe was happily employed for a decade in the aerospace industry in Los Angeles, consulting on satellite programs for the government. After earning an MBA from Stanford, Joe joined consulting firms Alphametric and then Netyear Group, where he wrote market research reports on Internet technology markets and consulted to executives in large Japanese companies. Joe managed to make up for his lack of Japanese language skills with diligence, humor, and good manners. His expertise in Internet technology can be found, if you read Japanese, in the book *It's Internet Commerce, Sir*. Along the way, Joe was caught up in the dot-com boom and co-founded iMahal, a portal for India with a strong focus on college education and early career success. He now resides in Pennsylvania where he continues to perfect this workbook and his teaching skills.

The Workshop: Stanford Continuing Studies Program

This workbook was developed for a workshop in the Stanford Continuing Studies Program using the following name and description: Writing with Clarity and Power in the Workplace - Rather than another course to review proper English usage, this course will help you to learn why bad writing is bad and why good writing is good. You will experiment with simple but powerful writing techniques and you will exercise mental muscles you never knew you had. Writing well is easy, but only for those who move beyond what they learned in school. We were all taught English, but few of us were taught how to write well, especially for work. By the end of the day, you will be wondering, "Why didn't they teach me this in school?" In this engaging workshop you will discover new ways to start with purpose, spot common errors, revise for clarity, edit for flow, and engage your readers. You will participate in a logical sequence of topics: thinking, writing, editing, usage, and style. Our workshop will culminate in candid discussions of how to spot and fix typical problems in email, letters, memos, reports, and briefings.

Published by Proofread.com
Printed in the United States of America
ISBN: 1-889831-00-X

Contents

Praise from business leaders around the world:

Joe Judge should be commended for bringing something new and valuable to the corporate training world. His work and publishing experience give him authority on the subject. His passion for good writing in the workplace comes through in every lesson.

Srikant Datar, Professor
Harvard Business School

Write Better at Work is a user-friendly way to review and improve the most important skills used in business, writing skills, while not testing the average professional's attention span.

Rian Schmidt, President
Fine Brand Media

I am recommending this training material to everyone in my firm as well as to my friends and colleagues.

Kiyo Oishi, COO
ACCESS Systems America

A valuable, practical, and easy-to-use tool for anybody writing anything as part of work or school.

Francisco Ceballos, CEO
MercadoLibre (Mexico)

The workbook offers practical communication tips and advice that would certainly make every employee of an organization a better communicator. This training material would be a great help to save everybody's time and improve company productivity significantly.

Sri L. Palasamudram, VP
VoiceWeb Corporation

The workbook guides us as we experience the complete processes of good business writing. It not only guides us how to write, but also teaches us how to think through our writing in a structured way. This is a great workbook to learn business English writing, even for non-native English speakers.

Shinichi Tonomura, Managing Director
Headstrong (Japan)

Part 1

Lessons

INTRODUCTION

Bob and Ben work in an office. Maybe it's an office just like yours, with cubicles and fluorescent lights. If you worked in this office and you went to get some coffee or water you might hear Bob and Ben trading advice about writing. We hope you enjoy their banter.

Notes:

To learn this material well, we recommend the following:

- Use a pen or pencil to scribble all over this workbook. Thinking while reading uses one side of the brain; writing while thinking engages the other side. Doing both together gives a result that is greater than the sum of the parts. It's how we learn best.
- Try the exercise in each lesson. Solutions are provided in the back of the workbook.
- Try the quiz at the end of the lessons. Answers are provided so you can grade it yourself.
- After you finish the lessons and the quiz, work through the practice material at the end of the workbook. Make as many mistakes as you can; you will learn more that way.
- If you are using this workbook as part of a workshop, remember: this is a time and place to relax and experiment. Be bold and don't worry about making mistakes. Class participation is not only encouraged, it is essential to getting the most out of it.

> If you would not be forgotten, as soon as you are dead and rotten,
> either write something worth reading or do something worth writing.
>
> *Benjamin Franklin*

THINK	AFFIRM	Resolve to not be part of the problem.
	DECIDE	Make sure it makes sense to put it in writing.
	DEFINE	Simplify your subject; put action in your purpose.
	DESCRIBE	Ask and answer to describe your reader.
	DEPICT	Draw your reader reading to get the picture.
	BRAINSTORM	Let your mind go to work in a cluster.
WRITE	OPEN	Give the reader a road map.
	PERSUADE	Primacy and recency have their place.
	ORGANIZE	Start early: be a diplomat and be a director.
	OUTLINE	Assemble your thoughts with purpose.
	DRAFT	Write fast, edit later.
	REST	Get perspective as the unconscious works.
EDIT	JUDGE	Obey rules, but be open to opinions and usage.
	CLARIFY	Ponderous writing is a choice: do the right thing instead.
	ALIGN	For clarity, align grammar to the story.
	GUIDE	Good flow uses transitions and links.
	VARY	Sentence length and format: the tools of greatness.
	ENGAGE	Write pithy hooks to keep enticing the reader.
	PROOFREAD	Make it correct with a trick, a printout, or a buddy.
USAGE	APOSTROPHE	It is (it's) best to use a memory device.
	COMMA	Use the comma, but do not give the reader pause.
	HOMONYM	Alliteration or rhyme: you'll have it for all time.
	VERB	Play Line & Link to match noun and verb.
	PRONOUN	Readers falter at limbo, mismatch, and shift.
	MODIFIER	Place them well, or readers frown and backtrack.
	PARALLEL	Repeating forms resonate with your reader.
STYLE	PASSIVITY	Write with vigor, or be a has been written.
	WORDINESS	Accelerate reading by doing a lot of deleting.
	IMPRECISION	Be precise to entice; details are nice.
	NEGATIVITY	Be positive. Use fewer nots.
	DRIVEL	Use spice sparingly, or be trite erringly.
	VANITY	It's not about you. Talk about the reader.
	BIAS	Be sensitive to gender, race, age, and disability.
FORMS	EMAIL	Write the message first. Control your emotions.
	LETTER	Be formal with strangers. Use full thoughts.
	RESUMÉ	To get noticed, make it action packed and error free.
	MEMO	Memos last: avoid embarrassment; write them well.
	REPORT	The best reports start with ideas on a pyramid.
	PRESENTATION	Keep it brief and consistent. Use the right graphic.

THINK: AFFIRM

Take-away:

Bad writing is everywhere. We are all part of the problem: we tolerate it every day.

Notes:

I wonder whether what we are publishing now is worth cutting down trees to make paper for the stuff.

Richard Brautigan

Below is an example of bad writing.

Recording illnesses has historically been a problem for employers, especially chronic or long term latent illnesses. This table is furnished to assist employers in making accurate illness determinations.

OSHA Record Keeping Guidelines, Appendix C

As we read it, our mind bothers us with odd questions: Is *recording* a verb or an adjective? Isn't *historically* redundant? Chronic employers? What is a *term illness*? Are companies actually allowed to find out about latent illnesses? What else is the table furnished with, silverware? Are employees determined to be ill? Why did the emphasis change from recording to determining? Is this really about observing, or is it about judging?

Finding examples of bad writing in government publications is like fishing in a barrel. It's too easy. We should recognize, however, that the problem is not limited to government. In a 1999 survey of 4,000 businesses, more than half said that the majority of their employees had deficient writing skills. One survey found that 30% of business letters are written by people who need to ask what was meant by the wording of a prior letter.

What is the cost of bad writing? "Ten percent of sales!" Seriously, many executives give this round number from their real-world experience. And that only estimates lost opportunities; it does not include losses in productivity. Consider the software industry and a product that is released with poorly written documentation. Here are just some of the problems that lead to increased costs:

- Increase in product returns.
- Increase in calls to the service center.
- Decrease in repeat business as customers get irritated.
- Decrease in credibility as angry customers complain to friends.

See if you can guess the answer to the following question.

Question: What are the most common excuses for tolerating bad writing at work?

(A) Public education should have taught our people enough English.

(B) We bought computers, so they should be helping.

(C) It's too difficult to assess the cost of bad writing.

(D) Writing well is hard work and time consuming.

(E) All of the above.

Unfortunately, to get the correct answer all you have to do is assume the worst. The take-away says it all. We should affirm to avoid being part of the problem.

THINK: DECIDE

Take-away:

Sometimes it's better *not* to put something in writing.

Notes:

Once a word goes out of your mouth, you can never swallow it again.

Russian Proverb

In the space below, write in a brief memo:

1. A description of a recent frustrating event at work, and
2. What you would like to see done about it.

Use no more than 5 sentences, and take only 2 minutes to write it.

Memo: Frustration and Solution

____

____

____

____

____

____

Now, for each of the five questions below, select Yes, Maybe, or No as your answer.

	Yes	Maybe	No	
Do I have a good reason for writing this?				I might be just venting or trying to impress.
Am I the right person to write this?				They might prefer to hear from another.
Is this the right time to be writing it?				It might be too dynamic at work right now.
Should I really put it in writing?				Once I write it, I can't take it back.
Is this preferred to verbal delivery?				Facial feedback could influence what I say.

Based on these answers, should you seriously consider perfecting and sending your memo? If you did not check off the entire Yes column, you have reason to stop right there. If you said Yes to everything, but had a nagging voice inside you saying, "well, maybe that one is a Maybe," then you have good reason to pause.

THINK: DEFINE

Take-away:

Make it a habit to write a purpose any time you write a subject.

Notes:

There are no dull subjects. There are only dull writers.

H. L. Mencken

Many people believe that writing is an act of improvisation. This mistaken belief contributes to procrastination and lazy thinking. It is the first step on the path to bad writing. The first step on the other path, the one to good writing, starts with a simple exercise in planning: writing down the subject *and* the purpose. Choose something you wrote recently: an email, a memo, or a report. Write down the subject and the purpose:

Subject:

Purpose:

Consider some new guidelines for writing a subject and a purpose:

Subject:
Use five words or fewer, but do not use any verbs or verb-like constructions.

Purpose:
Write one brief sentence. Begin with one of the four verbs, identify the reader, and include an instance of a suitable object.

verb	↔	reader	↔	object
inform	↔	Bob	↔	facts
instruct	↔	Bob	↔	tasks
motivate	↔	Bob	↔	behaviors
persuade	↔	Bob	↔	decisions

Example:			
	unclear	Subject:	All employees must begin the workday at 9 AM
		Purpose:	Complain about Bob being late to work all the time.
	concise & clear	Subject:	Tardiness
		Purpose:	Motivate Bob to show up on time.

Now take the second step on the path to good writing. Be more concise and clear by rewriting the subject and purpose according to the new guidelines:

New Subject: (use no verbs)

New Purpose: (use verb and object)

Ponder the result. Would you have written the document differently? This simple but powerful writing habit is useful for several reasons:

- It promotes early scribbling to generate ideas.
- It separates subject from purpose to encourage clear thinking.

THINK: DESCRIBE

Take-away:

Describe your reader reading: use words if that's how you visualize best.

Notes:

There's only one person a writer should pay attention to. It's the reader.

William Styron

When was the last time you stopped yourself from writing something so that you could first think about your reader? "Oops! I forgot to do a thorough analysis of my reader. I just can't write well without doing that first." Uh huh, we thought so.

Assessing the reader is like flossing: we know it's beneficial, but we don't do it as often as we should. Teachers told us to do it, but they seldom forced us to try it. Well, here is your chance to actually give it a try. Don't worry, it will all be over before you know it.

The task is this: visualize your reader in the act of reading what you have written. Okay, so how do we *visualize*? The key to getting the most benefit from the least amount of effort is to use the technique that is best suited to you. Some people work best with words; others work best with images. Let's first try a word-oriented approach: for the most recent significant thing you wrote at work, identify the reader and fill in a brief response about that reader in the table for each topic or question.

Who:	
Their job title and level of education.	
Their attitude towards me.	
What:	
What do they know about it?	
What should they do after reading it?	
Where:	
Where will they read it?	
Where are they in the hierarchy?	
Why:	
Why will they read it?	
Why would they react to it?	
When:	
When will they read it?	
When will they react to it?	
How:	
How interested are they in it?	
How will they be affected by it?	

Now ask yourself: Would this activity guide me to write in a way that makes it easier for the reader to get my message? If you answered No, you may be fooling yourself. There is always room for improvement.

THINK: DEPICT

Take-away:

Describe your reader reading: use images if that's how you visualize best.

Notes:

Thought is impossible without an image.

Aristotle

The other way to visualize your reader is to do it visually, using pictures. One approach is presented here, using stickpeople. Yes, that's right, stickpeople. The sillier the memory aid, the more effective it can be. Just have fun drawing something for each of the items in the diagram below.

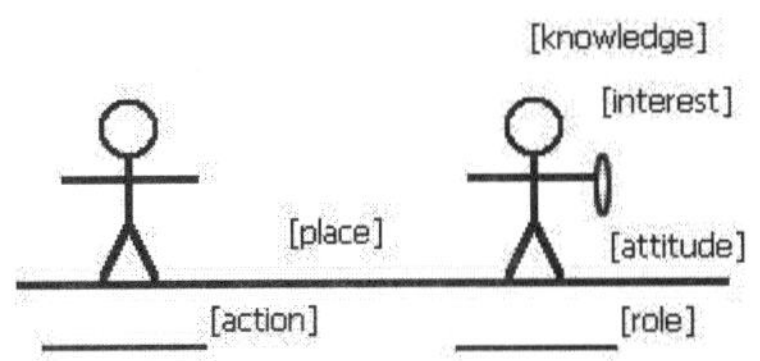

item	description	possibilities
action	What you want to do.	inform, advise, persuade
role	The role of the reader.	colleague, boss, customer
place	Where it will be read.	office, hotel, home
knowledge	What the reader knows about the subject.	big brain: expert small brain: ignorant
interest	How interested the reader is with the subject.	big ear: very interested small ear: indifferent
attitude	How the reader feels about you.	flowers: likes you cigar: indifferent dagger: out to get you

Here is an example:

You are writing to advise your boss. Your boss will read it at work (the desk). Your boss has extensive knowledge about the subject (big brain), isn't that interested (small ear), but thinks well of you (flowers).

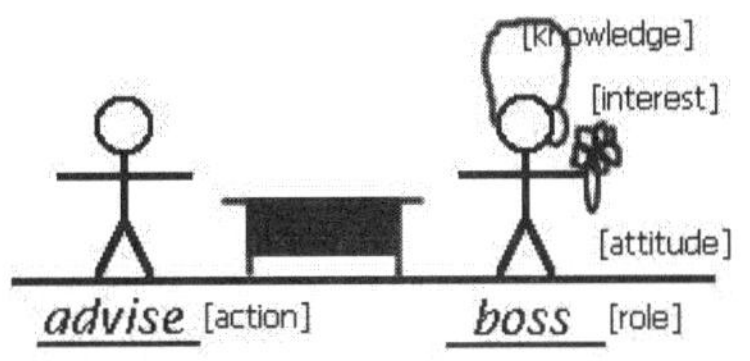

Use the diagram below. For a recent significant thing you wrote at work, write down two words, for the action and the role, and then draw fanciful images for the other items.

Draw your reader:

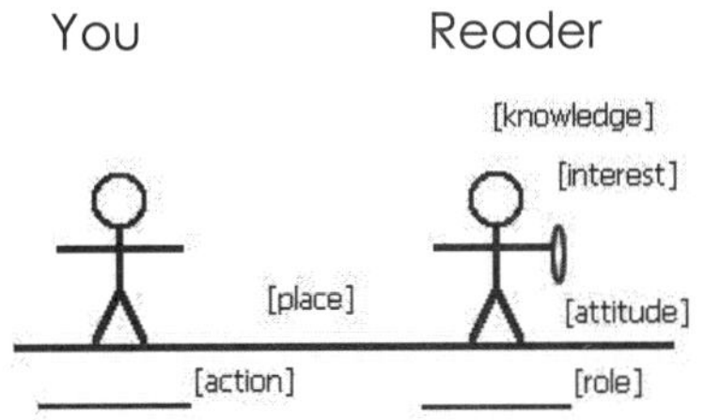

Again ask yourself: Would this activity guide me to write in a way that makes it easier for the reader to get my message?

Use your own pictures if you are image-oriented. Use your own list of questions if you are word-oriented. But, for the sake of your reader, visualize your reader reading your work. It will take just a few seconds.

THINK: BRAINSTORM

Take-away:

To jumpstart your writing, brainstorm with clustering.

Notes:

The act of composition is a series of discoveries.

E. L. Doctorow

Think back to when you received the offer for your current job. Now pretend you are writing an email accepting the job offer. Take a minute to think about it. Better yet, take three minutes, 180 seconds exactly, to play "word association" and to continue filling out the diagram below. Let your brain wander; make a new circle for each connecting thought that arises.

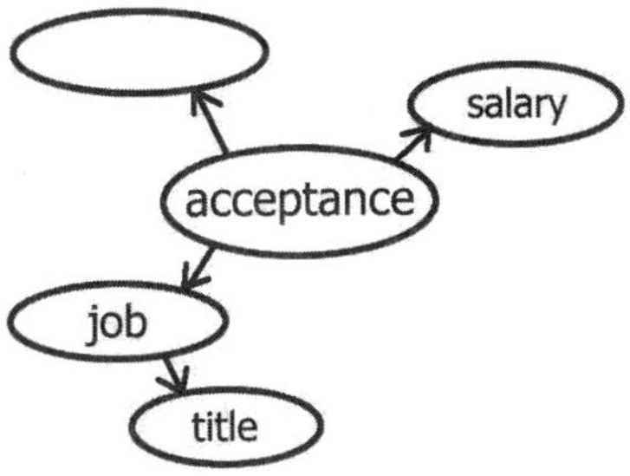

At what point in time did you feel like saying, "Okay, now I know what I want to write, so can I stop doing this?" Typically, this happens at about two minutes. How many circles are in your diagram? If there are fewer than ten you were not having enough fun.

This type of free association, sometimes called clustering or mind mapping, uses both sides of your brain: right for insight, left for logic. It also uses both levels of your psyche: unconscious for creating, conscious for refining.

When you draw a cluster, you map an interior landscape as your ideas emerge. It is effective because it reflects the way your creative mind works with thoughts and images: it groups things and it jumps, seemingly randomly, between groups. If you have trouble with clustering, it is most likely due to your conscious mind trying to stay in control. If this happens, just doodle by drawing connected circles, with nothing inside them. As you relax and continue, your conscious mind will step aside.

The Goal: When mind-mapping with clusters, the goal is not just the quantity of circles and quality of topics in the circles. More importantly, the goal is to identify things that you might otherwise have missed. For some writers the goal is also simply to jumpstart the writing process.

WRITE: OPEN

Take-away:

Every document should open with a brief introduction to the nature, issues, and findings.

Notes:

Well begun is half done.

Anonymous

The opening lines of documents we write at work are extremely important. A good opening is needed to ensure that our writing will be read instead of discarded. And, more importantly, a good opening is needed to give the reader a mental road map early in their journey through our document.

How not to write it: Far too often, we write openings using one of the following fallacies:

1. Any opening will do; I can wing it.
2. Everything I have to say is so useful, anything can go first.
3. Readers should experience it in the same sequence that I did.
4. To convince people, I must order things as I would in a mathematical proof.
5. To appear most professional, I should use the format of an academic research paper.
6. To avoid initial negative reactions, I should delay controversial findings until the end.

How to write it: The best techniques are the simplest. Here is how to do it:

- Write it early, expecting to modify it repeatedly.
- Write it as a separate thing, just as you wrote the purpose.
- Write it as a brief paragraph, intending to expand it later if needed.
- Consider it the verbal description you would give to the reader, who unexpectedly meets you in an elevator and asks what you are writing but has to get off the elevator after four floors.

What it should say: The opening of every document should include three components:

1. Nature - Clearly state the nature of the subject you are discussing.
2. Issues - Provide a preview of the main ideas you are presenting.
3. Findings - Introduce the conclusions or recommendations you are making.

The following opening will not help the reader much. Which fallacy does it use?

To decide whether to switch HMOs, a request was made for an independent review of your health plan. The HR department selected the author to interview employees and contact alternative HMOs. Access to HMOs proceeded smoothly; they were very receptive and eager to negotiate favorable terms. It was only after these efforts that the author was able to interview employees; it took that long for the HR department to get buy-in from annoyed supervisors. After organizing data and analyzing alternatives, the author prepared this report and submits it for management review.

fallacy: ________________

Here is an opening that does help the reader, but it's missing a component. Which one?

The purpose of this memo is to recommend a change in dental plans. We investigated who could provide adequate coverage at reasonable costs. There were difficulties finding a plan that met all our needs.

component: ________________

When you suspect or know that the gist of your document will not be what your reader wants to hear, you should use extra care in being tactful with your opening. Here are some phrases that can help:

- The findings are surprising.
- The problem is not X, as many people thought, but Y.
- The conclusion, which no one would have predicted given previous experience, is Z.

WRITE: PERSUADE

Take-away:

Think early about how you will order your ideas to best persuade your reader.

Notes:

Mere knowledge of the truth will not give you the art of persuasion.

Plato

Persuading the reader: Should you be concerned about this before you even do an outline? Absolutely. If you wait until you are editing, it will be more difficult for you and less effective for the reader.

To persuade people, use the concepts of **primacy** and **recency**. In the mind of your reader, the idea presented first has primacy and the idea presented last has recency. The ideas you state first and last have a better chance of being remembered than do the ideas placed in the middle. A good primacy message is, "I am one of you," and a good recency message is, "here is something to think about."

The example below shows six lines, in the order they occur, from a speech by Mark Antony in *The Tragedy of Julius Caesar* by Shakespeare. The funeral audience included a hostile group: supporters of Brutus, people Mark Antony wanted to discredit in the minds of the other funeral mourners. Use your imagination to write modern simple versions of what you think Mark Antony really meant as his primacy message and his recency message.

Mark Antony to the funeral audience:

	- primacy message -
• I come to bury Caesar, not to praise him	______________________
• The evil that men do lives after them	
• Brutus says he was ambitious	
• Brutus is an honorable man	
• You all did love him once, not without cause	- recency message -
• O judgment, thou art fled to brutish beasts	______________________

Here are other pointers for persuasive writing. Think of an adjective to complete each summary.

issue	**advice**	**summary**
Sides	For a hostile or ambivalent audience, always present both sides. For a friendly audience, use a one-sided argument.	Be ______________.
Facts	Giving many facts rarely changes attitudes; it only increases the resolve of those who already agree.	Be ______________.
Problems	If your views might cause problems for your readers, put extra effort into using empathy and tact.	Be ______________.
Testimonials	A testimonial is as effective as the source is "one of us."	Be ______________.
Recommendations	Credibility is enhanced if you include recommendations.	Be ______________.
Hyperbole	Credibility is diminished if you use hyperbole.	Be ______________.

WRITE: ORGANIZE

Take-away:

Organize early—be a diplomat and be a director.

Notes:

The difficulty is not to write, but to write what you mean, not to affect your reader, but to affect him precisely as you wish.

Robert Louis Stevenson

Early in the writing process, you should try to take on two roles: a diplomat and a director.

Diplomat: Organize your writing to be tactful. The effort you put into preparing your reader for your main point should vary directly with how much you think your point will make life difficult for your reader. As part of this effort, consider these general rules of diplomacy:

- When asking for something, give reasons before requests.
  Your opening will alert the reader to the nature of the request.
  State your reasons with as much detail as you think your readers are willing to read.
- When the topic is contentious, give details before conclusions.
  Giving details first at least gives you a chance to educate them.
  Giving conclusions early will only turn off those you really need to convince.
- When giving a refusal, explain before you refuse.
  This is most appropriate when the explanation is brief and you want to maintain future goodwill.
  Open with a neutral statement, give the explanation, give the refusal clearly, and end on a positive note.

Director: Organize your document so that readers will be so engaged that they can't put it down. A useful analogy is that your document is a movie and you are the director, implementing the activities below.

	activity	**analogy: result**	**analogy: role**
List:	identify all topics and ideas	a box full of photos	photographer
Sort:	put topics and ideas into groups	a photo album	designer
Order:	arrange groups by logical sequence	a movie	director

After gathering material, we organize it in three steps: list, sort, and order. The third step, ordering, is the one most often neglected by people in their writing at work. But it is the most important step for engaging the reader, who prefers carefully sequenced ideas in a document (or scenes in a movie).

In the example below, assume the opening will be used. Sort each item in the list by drawing a line to group A, B, or C, which have been given brief titles. Then, be a diplomat and a director: order the groups.

Opening: Maintenance of our website grew in difficulty, so we request that you increase our budget.

design of new website section $32,000 to outsource	1
peaks in website traffic jam the network	2
$45,000 for additional webmaster	3
one major update to a website section each month	4
$15,000 for artwork and proofreading	5
ten updated webpages promoted daily	6
publications department requires more budget	7
webmaster spends less time on intranet development	8
upgrade our network connection: $6,000	9
new sales division demands more assistance	10
network engineer monitors and reports on traffic	11
webmaster coordinates content development	12

A — requested budget increases

B — maintenance activities

C — maintenance difficulties

order: ☐ → ☐ → ☐

WRITE: OUTLINE

Take-away:

The best outline is a flexible list of brief statements that support your purpose.

Notes:

See first that the design is wise and just; that ascertained, pursue it resolutely.

William Shakespeare

Outlines grow up to be first drafts. This can be a good thing: it can keep you from wandering or getting stuck while writing your first draft. But it can also be a bad thing: flaws in the outline are typically preserved in the first draft. Four pieces of advice will guide you well in preparing an outline:

Use a template: It's natural and efficient to base your outline on a company template or a copy of someone else's document.

Use veto power: If the subject and purpose aren't fully supported by the format of the company template, give veto power to your subject and purpose. The template is only a guide; don't let it bully you.

Avoid one-word headings: When you are outlining, you should be generating possibilities, not summarizing. One-word headings restrict thought and look more like stop signs than green lights when you use the outline to write your first draft. Use brief statements for all headings in your outline. If company policy requires one-word headings, add them later.

Avoid the table of contents: Your writing plan starts to freeze when you use numbers and letters. Keep your outline flexible: use bullets and dashes.

For the outline below, assume the subject and purpose are accurate, and make the following changes:

- Delete irrelevant sections.
- Replace one-word headings with brief instructive sentences.
- Make it look less like a table of contents.

Subject: Computer virus security procedures
(Purpose: Instruct employees to avoid and kill viruses.)

I. History of the computer virus
    A. 1982 to 1998
    B. Recent IT woes
II. Consequences of a virus
    A. Productivity
    B. Intellectual property
    C. Reputation
III. Protect against a virus
    A. Employees
        1. Use a virus-scanning program
        2. Block executable code
        3. Make regular backups
    B. Departments
        1. Distribute security bulletins
        2. Audit anti-virus software
IV. Follow emergency procedures
    A. Isolate your computer
    B. Call the hotline

WRITE: DRAFT

Take-away:

Write the draft fast, expecting that it will be a mess in need of editing.

Notes:

Convince yourself that you are working in clay, not marble, on paper, not eternal bronze: Let that first sentence be as stupid as it wishes.

Jacques Barzun

Think about the most recent example of an important thing you wrote at work. For each of the four questions below, mark a spot on the line to give your best subjective answer.

When writing your first draft, how often did you stop to make **edits** to what you had already written?

never |———|———|———|———| often

How many writing **sessions** did it take to complete your first draft?

one |———|———|———|———| many

How did you feel about the **complexity** of the writing assignment?

confident |———|———|———|———| overwhelmed

How did you feel about the **deadline** for the writing assignment?

comfortable |———|———|———|———| oppressed

Of course the ideal spot on all four lines is the far left. But achieving this ideal is sometimes out of our control. Your employer typically controls deadlines, and your boss often controls complexity. You have some control over sessions but total control over edits.

The optimal way to write a first draft is this: *quickly write it all down before you change any of it.* The reasons are as follows:

1. **You will finish faster.** The draft/edit/edit way of writing is much faster than the write/edit/write/edit way of writing. This helps you schedule better to meet deadlines.
2. **You will feel better.** After completing the first draft, you will have a "whole document" view. This view gives you an understanding of how difficult it will be to write all later versions of the document. This reduces anxiety about complexity.
3. **You will edit better.** People who use the write/edit/write/edit pattern tend to consider the early sections of the document completed, and therefore do a lazier job of editing them in the final draft. Also, we edit better when we are more relaxed. By having a full first draft done, your sessions will be more relaxed because you will have less need to fret about complexity and deadlines.

To *quickly write it all down before you change any of it,* we offer the following advice:

- **Be directed but flexible.** Know where you are going by using an outline as a guide. Treat your outline as you would a map when on vacation: follow logical paths, but allow brief detours.
- **Be willing to write a first draft that has holes in it.** When you come to a spot where you are missing something (idea, data, graphic, quote), skip several lines and leave a note to yourself about what is to be inserted at this spot. Then skip a few more lines and continue immediately.

Above all, remember: the first draft *should* be a mess. If you write it without using an outline, it is likely to be a useless mess. If you write it using a good outline, it will be a useful mess.

WRITE: REST

Take-away:

After the draft, take a break from writing, knowing that the creative work will continue.

Notes:

> Theoretical insights flourish best when the thinker is apparently wasting time.
>
> *J. Robert Oppenheimer*

It was a dark and stormy night. I was writing like there was no tomorrow. Suddenly, a voice rang out, "Please sir, step away from the writing!"

We all need a writing cop—someone who tells us to stop once in a while. "Go home! Go sleep it off. Come back tomorrow." There are two reasons why we should be our own writing cop:

1. If we refuse to stop, we can get too close to the material and lose perspective.
2. When we stop writing things down, our unconscious has an easier time of continuing the writing and generating creative solutions to our writing problems.

In our dreams and daydreams, we recast our life incident by incident, into a form that pleases us. We reconstruct our activities and our conversations so that we are heroes. This unashamed reconstruction is often seeded by the conscious mind, by what is "foremost on our mind." And, like it or not, our work and our writing at work are often the things that are foremost on our minds. We might as well take advantage of this by giving our unconscious the time to give us some valuable off-line thinking for free.

So when should we do this? Actually, it happens by itself. Many writers and inventors have received their most creative insights when they were least expecting them, often while dreaming. In the examples below, draw a line to match each famous creator with the creation he dreamed.

creator		(dreamed)		creation
Samuel Coleridge, 1797	1		A	The periodic table.
Dimitri Mendeleyev, 1868	2		B	The song *Yesterday*.
Nikola Tesla, 1882	3		C	The manufacture of insulin.
Frederick Banting, 1920	4		D	The poem *Kublai Kan*.
Paul McCartney, 1965	5		E	The induction motor.
Patrick Brown, 1992	6		F	The gene chip.

Advertising guru James Webb Young said it well:

> "Out of nowhere the idea will appear. It will come when you are least expecting it—while shaving, or bathing, or most often when you are half awake in the morning."

Can you remember having a similar experience? This kind of sudden insight seldom arrives when you are trying to make it show up. Why not take advantage of this phenomenon by accepting rest as a natural part of your writing process? Some writers find it helpful to give hints to their unconscious:

'Tonight, come up with a creative solution to that report I am having difficulty writing.'

Give it a try; it only takes a few seconds. Say it but then forget about it. Let the unconscious work.

EDIT: JUDGE

Take-away:

Rules help us to understand each other, but they do not guarantee it.

Notes:

It is well to remember that grammar is common speech formulated. Usage is the only test. I prefer a phrase that is easy and unaffected to a phrase that is grammatical.

W. Somerset Maugham

Other than my boss, who should I obey regarding my writing?

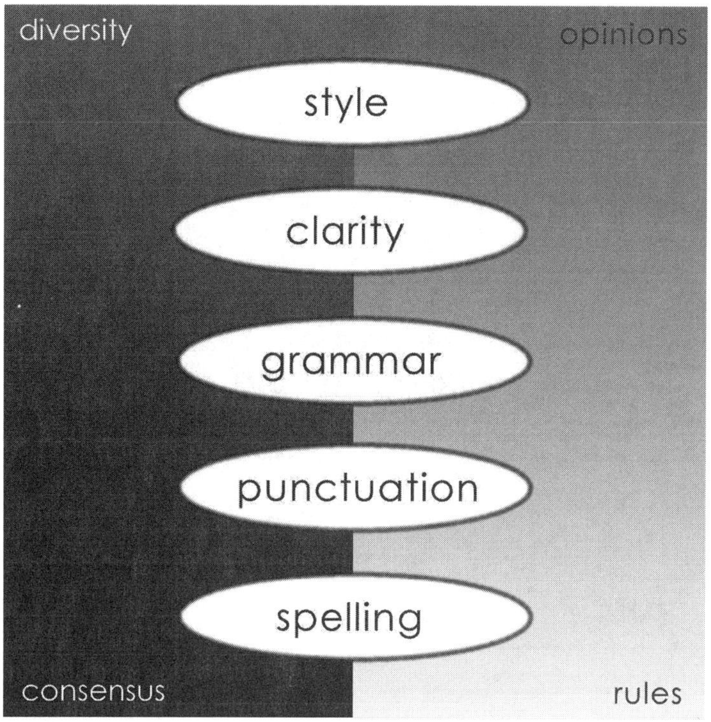

There is no single authority on good writing. Yes, the dictionary spells things out in black and white. But as the topic moves from spelling to grammar to style, rules become opinions with shades of gray.

In this workbook you will find both rules and opinions. They shouldn't be new to you. School teachers presented most lessons as rules, and colleagues are free with their opinions about how you should write.

The best thing to do is obey the rules and consider the opinions. It's your writing, so you are the sole judge.

However, there is a third source of authority in writing: usage. By this we mean how most people generally use English. And it is not always easy to figure out which authority should be followed. It's like the rock-scissors-paper game:

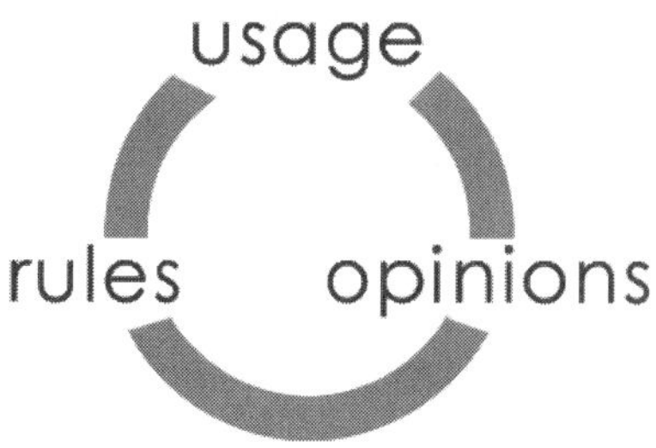

rock-scissors-paper ↔ rules-opinions-usage

Give an example of why the dictionary is not always the final authority regarding spelling.

Describe what Winston Churchill meant when he said: "This is the sort of errant pedantry up with which I will not put."

Explain what is wrong with the following pronouncement: "At work, *never* use a big word when a small word could be used."

At work, effective communication should outweigh grammatical purity. So, usage usually trumps rules.

EDIT: CLARIFY

Take-away:

Ponderous writing can be a habit in your profession, but it should be a habit you can change.

Notes:

In literature, the ambition of the novice is to acquire the literary language; the struggle of the adept is to get rid of it.

G. B. Shaw

Below are two examples of academic writing—abstracts from research papers. They were written by professors at the Stanford Graduate School of Business. On the line below each example, complete the sentence to summarize the issue for a CEO who has been advised to implement the idea proposed in the research paper.

This paper investigates how a designer of an organization (referred to as the regulator) should organize a production activity in which two different units produce components and where each unit has private information about its cost. Under informational decentralization, the optimal output schedule may not depend on the sum of the marginal costs of each components, but when it does, the regulator strictly prefers informational consolidation to informational decentralization.

1. It explains how to ____ .

A story often told informally is that in the context of repeated games, it may pay players to acquire reputations for such things as "toughness." If this reputation can be gained, then the opponents anticipate tough play and respond accordingly, yielding benefits that far outweigh the costs.

2. It explains how to ____ .

Which one of these examples was easier to read? If you had to choose one of the authors based on their writing, who would you hire to advise you?

Ponderous writing is a problem in most professions: academia, science, engineering, medicine, law, etc. Unfortunately, it is not just a bad habit that practitioners inherit. It is often considered part of the moral code within each profession. John Kenneth Galbraith said it well:

> "Complexity and obscurity have professional value—they are the academic equivalents of apprenticeship rules in the building trades. They exclude the outsiders, keep down the competition, preserve the image of a privileged or priestly class. The man who makes things clear is a scab. He is criticized less for his clarity than for his treachery."

If you are forced to write like this, then obviously you have no choice. But if you do have a choice, edit for clarity, not for conformity to the ponderous style of others in your profession.

EDIT: ALIGN

Take-away:

Reading is easier when the grammar aligns with the story.

Notes:

Writers know what they intend to mean, but only readers know what a passage actually means.

Joseph Williams

Read the following two sentences, and decide which one you like better:

> The engineer's conclusion was that a failure of the network will happen tomorrow.
>
> The engineer concluded that the network will fail tomorrow.

Most people like the second sentence better, but why? "The second one is more clear." Okay, but what does that mean? How do we recognize when a sentence is not clear? And how do we change it to make it clear? The answers to these questions all involve the concept of *alignment*. Every sentence we write is being read twice: in the reader's brain there is a grammar reader and a story reader. The grammar reader follows the structure of the sentence. The story reader follows the meaning of the sentence. Alignment occurs when the story matches the grammar. It is this alignment that makes sentences "more clear." Here is the breakdown of story and grammar for the misaligned, and therefore unclear, version:

The engineer's conclusion was that a failure of the network will happen tomorrow.

	main clause			subordinate clause			
grammar:	subject:	conclusion	verb:	was	subject:	failure	verb:	will happen
story:	actor:	engineer	action:	concluded	actor:	network	action:	will fail

Using the story, we can rewrite the sentence to get the aligned, and therefore clear, version:

The engineer concluded that the network will fail tomorrow.

	main clause			subordinate clause			
grammar:	subject:	engineer	verb:	concluded	subject:	network	verb:	will fail
story:	actor:	engineer	action:	concluded	actor:	network	action:	will fail

To create alignment:

1. Identify the actor—ideally a person or thing—and make it the subject.
2. Identify the action of the actor and make it the verb.
3. Rewrite the sentence based on the new subject and verb.

In the following sentence, identify the actors and their actions, then align the grammar to the story.

Our consultant's understanding is that arguments by managers were frequent.

actor: ______________ action: ____________ actor: ____________ action: ______________

____

Writing that people call ponderous is often caused by the purposeful misalignment of story and grammar. It is typically justified by "a need to appear objective." This is a bad excuse, not a good reason.

EDIT: GUIDE

Take-away:

Readers like to be guided with transitions and links.

Notes:

I sometimes think that writing is like driving sheep down a road. If there is any gate to the right or left, the readers will most certainly go into it.

C. S. Lewis

Does it flow? Is it easy to follow? These are subjective issues. But because it is important to your reader, it should be important to you. The most powerful techniques are also the easiest to implement:

Pronouns: Where there is a persistent subject in a paragraph, use pronouns as much as possible, but only when there is no ambiguity as to what each pronoun refers to.

Transitions: Between related paragraphs, place a transition sentence to connect them.

	how to do it	example
amplify:	Repeat a key word or set of words.	... project managers ... | Project managers also ...
contrast:	Show differences between things.	... project A expanded ... | Project B, though, shrunk ...
emphasize:	Restate a key idea in a different way.	... project was delayed ... | As the schedule slipped ...
expand:	Show an additional aspect of an idea.	... causes project overruns ... | Overruns are not the only thing ...
question:	End with a question; start with an answer.	... So which project succeeded? | Project A was the winner ...

Links: When a paragraph has related sentences, link them using extra words that guide the reader.

compare:	in comparison, in the same way, likewise, similarly
concede:	certainly, granted, naturally, of course, to be sure
conclude:	as a result, finally, in conclusion, lastly, to sum up
contrast:	although, however, in contrast, nevertheless, on the other hand, yet
deduce:	accordingly, as a result, consequently, hence, so, therefore, thus
elaborate:	after all, also, besides, for example, furthermore, in addition, moreover, specifically
emphasize:	above all, indeed, in fact, most important
order:	afterward, before, first, second, next, formerly, subsequently, then
place:	adjacent to, here, in the distance, in the front, near, next to, there

In the paragraphs below, improve flow by doing the following:

- Replace a long noun phrase with a pronoun in the first paragraph.
- Insert a transition sentence at the beginning of the second paragraph, repeating a key word.
- Insert links at the beginning of sentences within the second paragraph, elaborating on the transition sentence.

Collection-type heritage assets acquired in fiscal 2000 amounted to $61 million. The public entrusts the government with collection-type heritage assets and holds it accountable for their preservation.

The Library of Congress holds the world's largest library collection: 115 million items. The Smithsonian Institution holds 140 million objects for public exhibition. The National Archives holds 2 million cubic feet of records, including the U.S. Constitution.

EDIT: VARY

Take-away:

Keep readers interested: vary sentence length and format.

Notes:

Generally, style becomes perfect as it becomes natural—that is, colloquial.

A. R. Orage

Most people adopt a lifelong habit of writing most of their sentences in one preferred length and one preferred format. But one thing that separates great writers from good writers is variety in sentence length and format. Use variety to keep your readers interested:

Length: Vary the length of your sentences. In most writing at work, sentences should be between 5 and 25 words long. If most of your sentences are about the same length, you should interject some variety, especially if the average length exceeds 20.

Format: Vary the format of your sentences: highlight important points at the beginning, middle, and end of your sentences.

Beginning: To make a point, start with a prepositional phrase.

Middle: Place words—between dashes—to interrupt and inform.

{to do this with Microsoft Word: Insert → Symbol → Special Characters → M dash}

End: Place an example after a colon: like this.

In the paragraph below, add variety to each sentence:

- Start sentence 1 with a prepositional phrase.
- Condense sentence 2 down to a 5-word statement.
- Insert an interruption to highlight a strong point in sentence 3.
- Put an example word at the end of sentence 4.

We were able to find out what people thought about the cafeteria with a detailed survey. We tallied the results and discovered a trend in opinions of users that was not surprising. The menu was considered to be monotonous to the point of torture by every single respondent. Cafeteria managers were finally able to learn that variety is the key to pleasing their customers.

- ____
- ____
- ____
- ____

If you will notice, we started with a monotonous writing pattern: four standard sentences—each sixteen words long. What we ended up with is much more interesting to read.

EDIT: ENGAGE

Take-away:

Use hooks to repeatedly engage your reader.

Notes:

Everything which is written is meant either to please or to instruct. This second object is difficult to effect without attending to the first.

Sidney Smith

To keep the reader engaged, you should write every "beginning" to entice the reader, over and over again. Otherwise the reader may lose interest. Each beginning—title, abstract, heading, initial sentence in a paragraph—should hook the reader. Ideally, it should describe where we are and hint at where we are going. Here are some of the actions that hook readers:

- give a summary
- give a definition
- give a description
- make a prediction
- quote someone
- ask a question
- tell a story
- tell a joke

A good way to develop the ability to write hooks is to pretend you are writing the words for a roadside billboard. It must be brief, and it must grab the attention of the reader who is speeding by.

Assume the sentence below summarizes a section in a report. Now assume you need to write a heading for that section. Write pithy hooks that capture some of the essence of the sentence. Try to use fewer than nine words for each one. Creative thinking like this will help you write enticing beginnings.

General Frank explained that the After Action Review (AAR) is a professional discussion of an event, focused on performance standards, that enables participants to discover what happened, why it happened, and how to sustain strengths and improve on weaknesses.

definition: ______________________________

prediction: ______________________________

quote: "AAR tells it like it is." -General Frank

question: ______________________________

story: The general let'em have it at the AAR.

joke: ______________________________

Wording matters, especially when we want not just to engage the reader, but to get the reader to respond to us, in the real-world sense. The response rate increases dramatically when we avoid putting road-blocks in front of our imperatives. Write directly to get results. On the right, get rid of the "if" to create a final, brief, engaging version.

If you have any questions, you may contact me at any time.

*

Contact me if you have any questions.

*

____

EDIT: PROOFREAD

Take-away:

Proofreading is best done on paper and by a friend.

Notes:

Half my life is an act of revision.

John Irving

Proofreading is like combing your hair. If you don't do it, you will look sloppy. Your comb, like a spellchecker, is necessary but not sufficient. Your mirror doesn't show every part of your head, so you need to find a way to identify every imperfection.

Try these two techniques that professional proofreaders are said to use:

Use a straight edge: Using a piece of paper, cover up all but the first line of the paragraph below. Circle the errors you find. Then uncover the next line and continue.

I need you're advise. Your my "guru of goop.' Their maybe trouble with the mixture. Should'nt we package it in plastic. Its like mashed potatos. It will travel by plain, than by train.

Go backwards: Using a pen or your finger, point at the final word of the paragraph below. Play "follow the bouncing ball" and go left and then up a line, pointing at every word in the paragraph in reverse order. Circle the errors you find.

This work enviroment is like a race coarse it's frantic and loud. Wouldn't you like some piece an quiet. This weak we should'nt be hear. But a brake from the action might be to much to ask four.

How many errors did you find using each technique? There are twelve errors per paragraph, evenly distributed among sentences. Some people find the straight edge technique useful for grammar and the backwards technique useful for spelling. But, to be honest, few people find either technique very useful.

Now you know: *there are no shortcuts.*

Two other simple habits are your best bets for catching those embarrassing mistakes:

Use hardcopy: Editing a document on a computer can cause anxiety; we get tense when we spend a lot of time typing on a keyboard and staring at a screen. We edit better when we are relaxed, and we are more relaxed when we sit back and hold paper as we edit the text printed on it.

Ask a buddy: Even the best of friends love to find fault; use it to your advantage.

USAGE: APOSTROPHE

Take-away:

To remember how to use the apostrophe, it's helpful to use a mnemonic device.

Notes:

Reserve the apostrophe for it's proper use and omit it when its not needed.

*William Safire**

*note: He was joking.

Apostrophes are used for three main reasons, as described below, but we will concentrate on the one use of the apostrophe that many people get wrong.

Signal contractions: I'd do it, but he won't.

Show possession: Diane's company's profits are hers to spend.

Form plurals without ambiguity: Mind your p's and q's in the 1990s.

The sentence below needs an apostrophe. Where does it go? Should it signal a contraction? (short for *it is*) Or should it show possession? (the apostrophe would indicate something belongs to *it*)

Its an odd parrot that mimics its own voice.

Apostrophes are not used with the possessive forms of personal pronouns: *his*, *hers*, *its*, *yours*, *ours*, *theirs*. The possessive case is already built into the word. This is not the case for impersonal pronouns: *one's*, *nobody's*, *anybody else's*.

The main problem with this is the frequency with which we use the constructions *its* and *it's*. Many people either toss a coin to pick one, or just always use *it's*, settling for being correct half the time. It's not necessary—there is a solution. The key to always getting it right is to find a memory aid that works for you. Examples are given below.

Squeeze the *i* and leave the dot.

Pretend to squeeze the phrase *it is* until the bottom of the second *i* drops out to form the contraction *it's*.

The *s* belongs to the *t*.

For the possessive case, make the *s* belong to the *t*, with nothing in between them.

It's not like yours.

The contraction (of *it is*) is not like the possessive personal pronoun, which does not use an apostrophe.

His, hers, its.

Possessive personal pronouns do not use the apostrophe.

USAGE: COMMA

Take-away:

Readers are guided by commas, so use them liberally but carefully.

Notes:

Anyone who can improve a sentence of mine by the omission or placing of a comma is looked upon as my dearest friend.

George Moore

How often do you put a period in the wrong place? Or forget to use one? Most likely never. Now ask yourself the same question about the comma. Most people think, "Of course I obey the rules about using the period, but the use of the comma is a subjective thing." The problem with this reasoning is that there is nothing subjective about it for the reader. If the reader is forced to retrace or falter, even for an instant, then you aren't using commas properly. The four most common problems in using the comma are described below; use them to fix the comma problems in the sentences that follow.

Introductory element: Use your ear to decide if a comma is needed after an introductory element; if in doubt, put in the comma.

unclear: Clueless as always Bob broadcast the email.
clear: Clueless as always, Bob broadcast the email.

Compound sentence: If two complete sentences are joined by a conjunction, always put a comma in front of the conjunction.

wrong: Bob broadcast the email but Ben deleted the virus.
right: Bob broadcast the email, but Ben deleted the virus.

Comma splice: If two complete sentences are joined by a comma, always include a conjunction after the comma.

wrong: Bob needed office supplies, there were plenty in the cabinet.
right: Bob needed office supplies, and there were plenty in the cabinet.

Series separator: Always play it safe by putting a comma between every pair of elements in a series. The typical reason for not doing this is the complaint, "Journalists don't do it, so why should I?" Ask them why they do it and they will talk about tradition, not about clarity. You will never be unclear if you include all the commas.

fuzzy: Bob needed folders, pens and paper.
clear: Bob needed folders, pens, and paper.

Nikola Tesla invented the induction motor but electric resonance was his passion.

1. ☐ introductory element ☐ compound sentence ☐ comma splice ☐ series separator

Charles Steinmetz expanded our knowledge in hysteresis, modeling and lightning.

2. ☐ introductory element ☐ compound sentence ☐ comma splice ☐ series separator

Discovered by Michael Faraday electromagnetic induction electrified the world.

3. ☐ introductory element ☐ compound sentence ☐ comma splice ☐ series separator

Thomas Edison tried his best, his direct-current systems lost out.

4. ☐ introductory element ☐ compound sentence ☐ comma splice ☐ series separator

Notice that we didn't delete a comma in any of these examples. Most people under-use the comma.

USAGE: HOMONYM

Take-away:

Create silly memory aids, and you won't have to look up homonyms forever.

Notes:

Words are all we have.

Samuel Beckett

Homonyms are words that are pronounced the same but have slightly different spellings and often have very different meanings. The spellchecker is not your friend when it comes to homonyms. It will give you a false sense of security about the correctness of your writing. The only solution is diligence. You must be diligent in memorizing how to properly use homonyms, and you must be diligent in looking for them in your writing.

In the sentence below, circle the correct homonyms to use.

The acquisition will complement/compliment our product line and please our principle/principal investor, but it will also adversely effect/affect morale.

Words don't have to sound exactly the same for people to be confused about them. Circle the correct word in the choices below that sound similar.

Some managers were adverse/averse to our plan to assure/ensure that we would have continuous/continual performance reviews.

These are the homonyms and "almost homonyms" that people most often use incorrectly. The best way to learn proper usage is to invent a memory device. Use one from below, or make up your own.

affect: influence (verb) effect: result (noun) effect: cause (verb)	Air affects aardvarks; eels effect electricity.
complement: complete compliment: praise	To complement is to complete.
principle: truth principal: main, chief	The principal is your principal pal.
adverse: harmful averse: opposed	Avis is averse to adverse ads.
assure: convince ensure: make certain	I assured my assistant, who is since convinced.
continuous: uninterrupted continual: repeated	Our continual ball is in the fall.

USAGE: VERB

Take-away:

Make editing into a speed-reading game to find mismatches between subject and verb.

Notes:

Grammar is a piano I play by ear. All I know about grammar is its power.

Joan Didion

Let's play a game called Line & Link. Read *quickly* through the paragraph below, following these rules:

1. When you read a noun that appears to be the subject of the sentence or of a clause, underline it with a single line.
2. When you read a verb that looks like the main action of the sentence or clause, underline it with a double line. For a split second consider whether the verb matches the noun you underlined. If not, quickly circle the verb and move on.

Everyone in the organization, including my colleagues, understand that we want to maintain a learning culture. We believe that it is appropriate for humans to be proactive problem solvers. Each reality and truth about our working environment are pragmatically discovered. Accurate data and relevant information flows freely in a fully-connected network. Human nature, though presumed good for most people, are at least mutable. My group in Marketing and Sales believe that diverse but connected units are good for the organization. We also believe that we must allow for a diversity of task-oriented and relationship-oriented people.

This is an effective way to blast through your writing to find the most common verb problem: mismatched subject/verb pairs. Typically the problem will be with number. A singular verb should be matched with a singular subject; plural verbs should be matched with plural subjects.

There are seven sentences in the paragraph above. You should have found an error in all but two of the sentences. When you play Line & Link, what you are actually doing is using your ear and your short term memory to isolate and combine subject/verb pairs. In the first sentence, for example, you should have quickly selected and combined, *Everyone understand*, which should have triggered a nasty response from your grammar-trained brain.

Some people find it helpful to mumble nonsense syllables, such as "dah deh dah" or "yada yada," when reading quickly over the words in between the nouns and verbs. Use whatever works for you.

USAGE: PRONOUN

Take-away:

Every pronoun reference should be obvious, correct, and consistent.

Notes:

> The grammar is an attempt to make explicit and conscious what the speaker of English does intuitively and unconsciously.
>
> *Mark Lester*

The purpose of the pronoun is to make the reading go smoothly, by avoiding the repetition of nouns. However, if there is *ever* any doubt about what a pronoun refers to, the reader must stop for an instant and make a best guess. This defeats the purpose of the pronoun.

Spot pronoun problems by knowing what to look for. The three most common pronoun errors are:

Limbo: It is not obvious who the pronoun refers to.
example: Bob left the office to look for Ben, but he should be easy to reach.
(Whom does *he* refer to?)

Mismatch: The pronoun does not match (in person or number) the thing it obviously refers to.
example: Bob's cubicle was often home to impromptu meetings because they have a water cooler in front of them.
(The third person singular pronoun is appropriate: *it has .. it*.)

Shift: Bad parallel construction leaves one pronoun different from the others it should be similar to.
example: Each office on the floor had its own hookup to the Internet, a large window that made them bright, and an oak desk that made it elegant.
(All three phrases should use *it*.)

Among the sentences below, there is one instance of each of the three types of confusing pronouns. Make edits for clarity and then identify each type of error.

The consultants presented a detailed briefing about how it could advise the client.

1. ☐ limbo ☐ mismatch ☐ shift

My boss had a conversation with the attorney that caused her to modify her presentation.

2. ☐ limbo ☐ mismatch ☐ shift

I liked the creative maneuvering, the competition gunning for you, and the feeling that I was in a race to dominate the field.

3. ☐ limbo ☐ mismatch ☐ shift

Writing teachers sometimes recommend: "When editing, you should circle every pronoun and check that it agrees in person and number with its antecedent." If you have lots of time, this is an okay way to go. Otherwise, the thing to remember is that these confusing pronouns usually occur at the end of longer sentences.

USAGE: MODIFIER

Take-away:

Avoid making your readers have to interpret or move your modifiers.

Notes:

The other day I shot an elephant in my pajamas. (How he got in my pajamas I'll never know.)

Groucho Marx

Modifiers are words or phrases that act as adjectives or adverbs. They make our writing more specific, interesting, and memorable. But when we do a bad job of placing modifiers in a sentence, we confuse the reader. Entertainers use this confusion to create humor: "Speaking of names, I know a man with a wooden leg named Smith!" said Bert. "What's the name of his other leg?" asked Mary Poppins.

Bad placement of modifiers most often comes in one of four types:

Misplaced: It is not placed close enough to the words modified.
example: Bob insisted that we stop posting jokes about Ben on the coffee maker.
(Posting on the coffee maker? Or are we supposed to envision Ben sitting on the coffee maker?)

Squinting: It can refer to the words before it or to the words after it.
example: Bob remembered recently joking about Ben.
(Recently remembered? Or recently joking?)

Disruptive: It interrupts the connection between parts of the sentence.
example: The joke, because Bob insisted we display a modicum of office decorum, was taboo.
(Are you sure you want to put your reader on hold?)

Dangling: It modifies nothing in particular in the rest of the sentence.
example: Although a humorless boss, everyone kept telling that joke.
(Everyone is not the boss. Who is?)

Among the sentences below, there is one instance of each of the four types of troubled modifiers. Make edits for clarity and then identify each type of error.

The electricity, because the utility company was having trouble meeting peak demand, was unavailable for several hours.

1. ☐ misplaced ☐ squinting ☐ disruptive ☐ dangling

The accountant said she will need all departments to submit their budgets to her office at a meeting yesterday.

2. ☐ misplaced ☐ squinting ☐ disruptive ☐ dangling

As a new employee, his mentor told stories about the early days of the company.

3. ☐ misplaced ☐ squinting ☐ disruptive ☐ dangling

Programmers who change code repeatedly frustrate our project managers.

4. ☐ misplaced ☐ squinting ☐ disruptive ☐ dangling

Most people have trouble recognizing their troubled modifiers. The good news is that these modifiers are easily detected by others. Again, ask a friend to help you edit.

USAGE: PARALLEL

Take-away:

Prose without parallels is like music without rhythm: it can be easier to create, but is often harder to enjoy.

Notes:

Likeness of form enables the reader to recognize likeness of content.

William Strunk

Parallel construction is to prose what rhyme is to poetry. At least that's one way of looking at it. Readers are accustomed to having the benefits of parallel construction: fewer words, improved readability, and easier comprehension.

A common rule of grammar and rhetoric is that when we have groups of similar elements, we should coordinate them by assembling them side by side using a common grammatical structure.

Example:

chaotic: Bob <u>ate</u> lunch, <u>drinks</u> coffee, and <u>has fallen</u> over.
parallel: Bob ate lunch, drank coffee, and fell over.

Parallel construction should be used in a variety of ways: at the micro level (among clauses), at the middle level (among sentences), and at the macro level (among paragraphs and sections). We will practice spotting and fixing commonly-missed opportunities for parallel construction.

In the sentence below, two predicates are presented, but their structure is not parallel. It is much easier to read when they are similar in structure. Make it so.

The committee recommends spending the surplus on an office party and that next year's budget for entertainment expenses be increased.

In the next example, the items in the list should be grammatically parallel. If one element of a list is a complete sentence and it seems to read okay, then all elements should be complete sentences using a similar form. Make things parallel by rewriting two of the three bulleted items as imperatives.

Anyone requesting a change from last year's budget should follow proper procedures:

- Standard form only
- Include a detailed description.
- Your request should be submitted by Tuesday.

The final example is not just for parallel structure, but also for parallel thought. One of the elements in the sentence below is a thought that is not similar to the thoughts in the other elements. Break it out as a new sentence.

The auditor discovered mistakes in accounts receivable, found receipts that had not been recorded, corrected several ledger entries, and all this time our accountant could not be found.

STYLE: PASSIVITY

Take-away:

Passive voice numbs the mind of the reader: avoid it when you can.

Notes:

To write simply is as difficult as to be good.

W. Somerset Maugham

"Use active voice!" is the mantra of most teachers of clear writing. It's good advice, but how do we do this while editing? There are three ways to recognize passive voice and change it to active voice. All three focus on how to re-establish the subject of the sentence:

passive:	doee {is|was|..} Xed by doer	Ben was asked by Bob.	**transpose the subject**
active:	doer Xed doee	Bob asked Ben.	
passive:	in the A the B {is|was|..}Xed	In the file the job was listed.	**extract the subject**
active:	the A Xed the B	The file listed the job.	
passive:	it {is|was|..} Xed that C	It was decided that Bob must go.	**supply the subject**
active:	someone Xed that C	We decided that Bob must go.	

For the sentences below, change passive voice to active voice.

transpose the subject:

A problem with the server was isolated by Ben.

____

extract the subject:

In the access logs the source of the problem was identified.

____

supply the subject:

It was announced that the server had crashed.

____

Notice how passive voice forces us to write sentences that are longer and convoluted. If it takes you two seconds to comprehend a sentence written in active voice, it will typically take you three seconds to comprehend the same sentence when it is written in passive voice.

Use passive voice sparingly, and only in the following situations:

identity of the doer is unimportant	The network will be monitored.
doer is confidential	The file was destroyed accidentally.
doer is unknown	The system can be hacked.
to avoid being blunt	The network crash was caused by your emails.
to maintain flow	... These activities create a corrupted file. Corrupted files are isolated by network administrators ...

STYLE: WORDINESS

Take-away:

Avoid wordiness.

Notes:

The most valuable of all talents is never using two words when one will do.

Thomas Jefferson

Your readers are just like you: they are busy people, and they don't have all the time in the world. They want to get to the main point of your message quickly. So avoid wordiness. There are three things you can do when editing:

Delete deadwood: Get rid of words and phrases that are unnecessary. For example, there is seldom a good reason for beginning a sentence with *I should mention that.*

Sandblast bloat: Replace fancy words and phrases with simple equivalents. For example, you can usually replace *indication* with *sign*, and *banking facility* with *bank.*

Uncover buried verbs: This is most easily done by looking for words that end with *-ion*. For example, *make a suggestion* can often be replaced by *suggest.*

Remove the wordiness from the sentences below.

delete deadwood:

This letter is to advise you that your office is in the process of being cleaned; it should also be noted that extra work is required to be carried out on the carpets and drapes.

sandblast bloat:

In order to make it to the finalization of the project, you will need financial resources for emergency situations.

uncover buried verbs:

We have a suspicion that if you make a recommendation for leniency, they will come to the conclusion that our plan is not to raise an objection.

The debate on wordiness continues:

Rebuttal: Yeah, but what I'm writing is important, so I need the extra words and the formal phrases to make things perfectly clear.

Counter-Rebuttal: Hogwash. You don't need a lot of formal words to write important things. Only 462 words were needed to add the Bill of Rights to the Constitution—and that was written by lawyers.

STYLE: IMPRECISION

Take-away:

Keep readers interested by using lively verbs, unique nouns, and details.

Notes:

The difference between the right word and the almost right word is the difference between lightning and the lightning bug.

Mark Twain

Readers are bored easily. Boredom is not caused by looking at too much stuff; it is caused by looking at too much uninteresting stuff. When we write without precision—never saying precisely who is doing precisely what—our writing becomes dull. To avoid this, all we have to do is show things clearly by being precise. Here are three ways to do this:

Qualifiers: If they contribute nothing substantive, they are just bland placeholders. Get rid of them.

bland: Bob was very aware that someone was a little unhappy.
precise: Bob was aware that someone was unhappy.

Verbs and nouns: Generic products cost less at the grocery, and that is a good thing. But generic words cost you the reader's attention, and that is a bad thing. Use lively verbs and unique nouns.

boring: A study was used to find out about job satisfaction at our facility.
precise: A survey measured job satisfaction at our office.

Details: Vague statements bore people; specific statements interest them. Use details when you can.

vague: Job satisfaction has increased.
precise: Job satisfaction increased by 25%.

In the sentence below, cross out the qualifiers that stuff the sentence but do not make it any more satisfying.

Pretty soon we should be very alert to the rather odd way it gets a little worse.

In the next example sentence, replace verbs and nouns to make it more precise and interesting.

Money kept is money earned.

For the final example, assume you work at *The Economist* and you need to entice advertisers in the travel industry. Rewrite the sentence with relevant details, which you can make up for this example.

The Economist is one of the most read magazines in the world.

____

____

____

STYLE: NEGATIVITY

Take-away:

Make positives out of negatives so that readers willingly pay attention and easily comprehend your meaning.

Notes:

Apt words have power to suage the tumors of a troubled mind.

John Milton

There are two ways that negativity diminishes the impact of our writing:

Negative words: Certain words can trigger negative reactions in the mind of the reader. We begin to sound mean or pessimistic when we frequently use words with negative connotations, such as these:

allege	demand	fail	lack	problem	trouble
avoid	deny	fault	mistake	prohibit	unfair
bad	disapprove	ignorant	neglect	refuse	unreasonable
careless	eliminate	impossible	never	reject	unreliable
cease	error	inadequate	no	terrible	weakness
complain	exclude	inferior	not	trivial	wrong

negative: If you fail to pay this amount within 30 days, we will demand the balance and eliminate your account.

positive: Your account will stay open if you pay within 30 days.

Multiple negations: To comprehend a negative, people first imagine the positive and then cancel it out. Doing this too often, especially within one sentence, obscures meaning.

confusing: Interview not more than one candidate unless we haven't closed our hiring window.

clear: If we are not hiring, interview one candidate only.

For the example sentence below, underline the negative words and then rewrite this negative attack. Obviously this is subjective. Be creative, polite, and encouraging.

We demand that you cease complaining that the alleged problem was our fault.

____

Rewrite this sentence without the negations:

Managers should not ask for increased budgets unless they spent not less than 90% of last year's money.

____

____

STYLE: DRIVEL

Take-away:

Clichés, legalese, and buzzwords are okay, but only if used in moderation.

Notes:

We love to pump air into our language and make it soft and gaseous.

Edwin Newman

It's okay to spice up your writing at work. Just don't overdo it. A modicum of spice is just right when cooking; overloading on spices ruins the meal. Avoid being overzealous with the three worst forms of drivel:

Clichés: These are accepted, and even expected, by readers of newspapers. They are even acceptable in your writing at work. What is not acceptable is overuse of these clichés.

examples: in hot water (in trouble) hit pay dirt (succeed) run of the mill (typical)

Legalese: It is natural to feel the need to write like an attorney when writing something important at work. After all, that is what we are exposed to in the important documents at home, such as contracts and warranties. If you're not an attorney, avoid the temptation to write like one.

examples: cease and desist (stop) until such time as (until) render assistance (help)

Buzzwords: People who overuse pompous popular words give the appearance of trying desperately to stay employed. Maintain reader respect by avoiding overuse of these buzzwords.

examples: core competence (skill) leverage (use) incent (give incentives for*)

Write a new version for each of the sentences below, getting rid of the drivel.

Here is the long and short of it: heads will roll if we don't start from ground zero, hunker down, and pull out all the stops to crank it out.

____

It has come to our attention that pursuant to our prior conversation re this report it became necessary to attach herewith the appendix per your request.

____

Now write what people are likely to think when they hear drivel like this:

As an evangelist for the clicks and mortar paradigm here at Spacely Sprockets, I re-engineer enterprise knowledge management: that's my value add.

____

Here is a suggestion: write the way you would talk to your co-workers at a department picnic. They will respect the fact that you are willing to communicate with them like a normal human being would.

*yes, there are alternatives: entice, encourage, exhort, impel, incite, induce, motivate, spur, stimulate, urge, ...

STYLE: VANITY

Take-away:

Readers will pay better attention if you use the word *you* more than you use the words *I* or *we*.

Notes:

Remember that a person's name is to that person the sweetest and most important sound in any language.

Dale Carnegie

When you use a personal tone in an email, letter, or memo, you can make almost any subject more interesting to the reader. Also, when you write about the reader, not about yourself, you make your message truly engaging.

Always remember that your reader will be thinking:

- Why should I care about reading this?
- What does it have to do with me?

To help make the reader interested in what you have to say, write with two techniques in mind:

Converse: Have a conversation with the reader.
standoffish: It is our pleasure to introduce our new service.
conversational: You really might like our new service.

Mirror: Make the reader the subject of your sentences.
writer-oriented: We appreciate the efforts extended on our behalf.
reader-oriented: Thank you for helping.

The sentences below use unnecessary formality and a writer-oriented focus. Rewrite each of the three sentences in a way that is both conversational and reader-oriented. The best way to do this is to pretend you are talking face to face. Read your sentences out loud as if you were sitting with the reader, talking things over. Write the same way you speak. Talk to and about the reader.

I would like to extend an invitation to an upcoming seminar to learn about our services.

We put effort into streamlining our presentation so that your time will be well spent.

Call us if we can answer any questions you might have.

____

____

____

Exception: The use of the word *you* should be avoided when it can have a connotation of blame. In this case, change the focus to talk about groups or things:

reader-focus: You must not include sensitive data in your email.
group-focus: Employees must not include sensitive data in their email.
thing-focus: Email must not include sensitive data.

STYLE: BIAS

Take-away:

Sensitivity to bias is an essential attribute of writers who want to continue to be read.

Notes:

God send everyone their heart's desire.

William Shakespeare

Until the 1920s, women could not vote. Until the 1970s, women were barred from many jobs. Until our descendants do not frown at the phrase *she or he*, our language will continue to subtly exclude women from equal consideration. Gender bias problems include:

Pronouns: Avoid overusing the phrases *he or she* and *his or her*. Instead, use a plural pronoun, or rewrite the sentence. A plural pronoun with a singular subject is becoming accepted usage when it is used to avoid gender bias. It is the right thing to do, so our society is bending the rules.

awkward: The meal he or she orders should fall within his or her budget.
intelligible: The meal they order should fall within their budget.

Occupations: Choose an official replacement, or make one up.

businessman	→	business executive	fireman	→	firefighter
salesman	→	salesperson	mailman	→	mail carrier
congressman	→	congressional representative	foreman	→	supervisor
policeman	→	police officer	woman attorney	→	attorney

Name Differences: Be consistent with your references.

Mr. Tan and his wife Amy	→	Mr. and Mrs. Tan
Adam Lee and Ms. Eve Ward	→	Adam Lee and Eve Ward

People as a Group: Replacements are not hard to find.

mankind	→	people, humanity
man-made	→	synthetic
man-hours	→	work-hours
common man	→	average person

In addition to gender, there are other forms of bias to avoid, including race, age, and disability. The list grows as our society evolves. The only constant is the need for sensitivity.

Change this sentence before it subtly and adversely influences an impressionable reader, such as a niece:

Woodrow Wilson and his wife Edith agreed: the common man would be better off if every congressman voted his conscience about the 19th amendment.

____

____

Remove all possibilities of bias from this sentence:

Our young male nurse will meet with the black lawyer and the 52-year-old deaf engineer.

FORMS: EMAIL

Take-away:

Write and send emails with the same care that you write and send letters.

Notes:

I understand a fury in your words, but not the words.

William Shakespeare

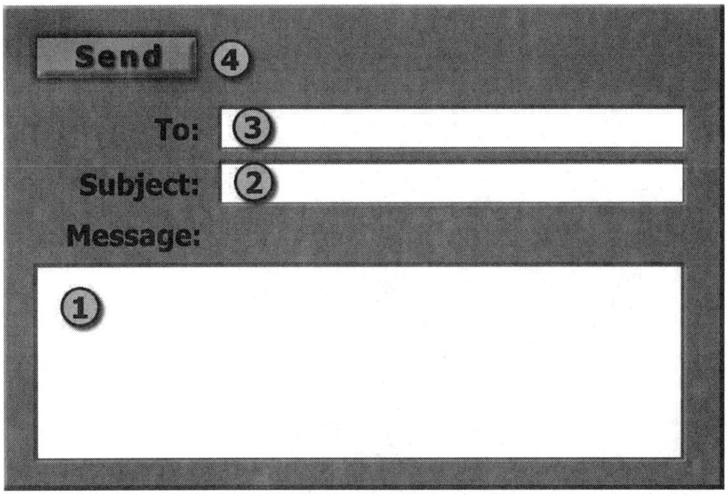

Treat your business emails like you treat your business letters: do not mail them until they are complete and polished. A good way to do this is to *always* type the message first. When the message is complete and polished, then type the subject. After this, type the recipient's email address. This habit has the added benefit that if you hit Enter or a Send button too early, you will not send the email before it's ready.

Write your emails so that they are both read and appreciated:

Subject line: Use it to succinctly summarize your message and to hook your reader. We all get too much email, so we all delete a lot of email based on what we see in the subject line.

Capital letters: Don't overuse them. USE ALL CAPS ONLY IF YOU WANT TO SCREAM!

Emoticons: Don't use them in business correspondence. ;-)

Emotions: Don't send emails when you are upset. Part of the power of email is that it's "real-time." If you don't *really* have to send that email now, wait awhile. Cooling off gives you needed perspective.

Informality: Anyone who writes an email like this, "hi - i heard u r done - plz send it ok? regds," is also saying, "you are not worth the effort for me to be professional and type using standard conventions."

Use these suggestions to rewrite the email below. Be nice. And be creative: give Bob guidance.

To: bob
Subject: way to go
Message: Your stupid email crashed the system because u broadcast it with a virus attached.
U SHOULD NEVER "REPLY TO ALL" ON A COMPANY-WIDE MAILING.
And, o yeah, r u incapable of turning on your virus-checking program? >:-@

Subject: ______________________________

Message: ______________________________

____

____

____

Also consider other issues unique to email:

Privacy: Assume every email can be read by people in charge of security in your organization.

Format: To make sure that the lines of your message are not all chopped up (long/short/long/short), do not hit the Enter key (new line) inside a paragraph. Let the email program do the formatting.

FORMS: LETTER

Take-away:

The best letters use simple words, full thoughts, and assertive endings.

Notes:

Gentlemen:
You have undertaken to cheat me. I won't sue you for the law is too slow. I'll ruin you.
Yours truly,

Cornelius Vanderbilt

Don't waste your time memorizing rules of format for letters. Look them up when you need them. Instead, put your effort into avoiding the four areas where people most often go wrong in business letters:

Inconsistent Formality: The salutation and the complimentary closing should match: be informal with friends, be formal with strangers and organizations, and be consistent.

salutation		complimentary closing	
Dear Bob:	informal	Kind regards,	Cheers,
Dear Mr. Rehme:			
Dear President:	↓	Sincerely yours,	Cordially,
Dear Board:			
Dear Academy:	formal	Yours truly,	Respectfully,

Is the phrase *To Whom It May Concern* acceptable? Yes, if you are writing an open reference letter, or if you are putting the letter in a bottle to be cast into the sea. Otherwise, use the name of the organization (for example, *Dear Academy:*)

Ponderous references: Avoid phrases like *above-mentioned* or *aforementioned.* It is unnecessary and puts the reader to sleep. Also, you can always find a better way to say *with reference to.*

Half thoughts: Avoid incomplete sentences, even when stating the subject of the letter. It will be read by a human, not a computer.

Weak suggestions: Most business letters should end with a call to action. Make it assertive and specific.

In the letter below, find examples of the four problem areas and suggest improvements.

Academy of Motion Pictures
8949 Wilshire Boulevard
Beverly Hills, CA 90210

Dear Academy:

With reference to the movie, *Evolution*, directed by Ivan Reitman. Please ensure that the Academy gives careful consideration to the aforementioned movie. Despite the unabashed product placement, it is a well-acted romantic action comedy. I hope you get a chance to view the movie by the end of the year.

Kind Regards,

Seann William Scott

Business letters are changing. The word *Dear* in a salutation has become optional. In many organizations, the salutation and complimentary closing are both no longer used. Below the salutation, or in place of it, a subject line has become an acceptable part of the business letter, making it more and more like a memo.

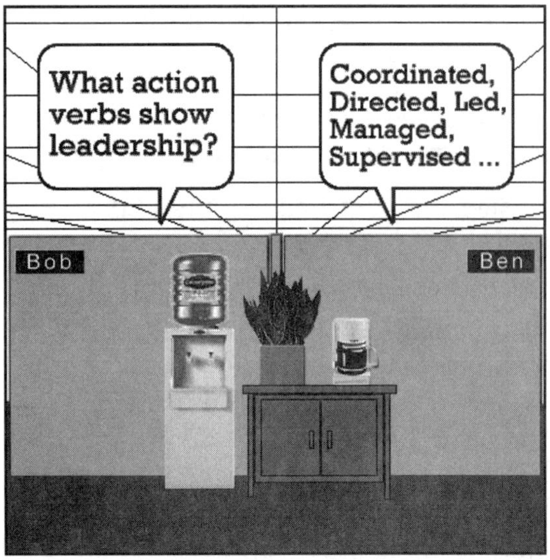

FORMS: RESUMÉ

Take-away:

Fill your resumé with active descriptions of capabilities and accomplishments.

Notes:

Believe in yourself. Have faith in your abilities. Without a humble but reasonable confidence in your own powers you cannot be successful or happy.

Norman Vincent Peale

Employers need to quickly answer two basic questions: Might the person represented by this resumé match our needs? Should I pass this resumé on to someone else in the company? Your job is to write your resumé so that they answer, "Yes!" Use the following 6 rules to correct the example below.

1. Use action verbs. The resumé is the worst place to use weak verbs or sleep-inducing passive voice.

weak verb and passive voice: Training seminars were put together for clear writing.
action verb and active voice: I organized seminars to train people to write clearly.

2. Use incomplete sentences. The subject, I (that is, you), is always implied.

complete: I organized seminars to train people to write clearly.
incomplete but preferred: Organized seminars to train people to write clearly.

3. Use the good stuff. Include only entries that highlight a capability or an accomplishment.

bland stuff: The company offered the negotiations seminar to new managers.
good stuff: Developed a negotiations seminar for new managers.

4. Avoid spelling errors. One error justifies throwing your resumé in the garbage can. It's that simple.

5. Avoid pompous fluff. Consider the following text: Self-motivated, hands-on team player with a proven track record in adding value. Now answer the question: Would *you* keep reading this fluff?

6. Avoid irrelevant data. Personal data (gender, age, race, health, marital status) present legal problems for employers; don't include it. Also omit social security number, salaries, and irrelevant associations.

Pat Ensenar

909 Cactus Blvd, San Antonio, Texas 88210 (909) 555-1212 patensenar909@hotmail.com

EXPERIENCE

Training Coordinator, St. Mary's College, San Antonio, Texas 1996 - 2002

- Enrolled employees in training classes and prepared facilities for presentations.
- A new class in conflict resolution was set up for department administrators.
- Employee participation in training classes varied with staff size.

Assistant Manager, Barnes & Noble Bookstore, San Antonio, Texas 1992 - 1996

- I managed inventory for books, music CDs, calendars, and magazines.
- Lead book discussion groups and arranged author events.

EDUCATION

Diploma, San Houston High School, San Antonio, Texas 1992

ACTIVITIES

Train tutors for Literacy Volunteers
Religious Advisor, Hash House Harriers of San Antonio

Here are a few more important issues to consider when writing your resumé:

Length: One page is ideal, especially with fewer than 5 years experience. Never more than 2 pages.

Scanning: Make your resumé scanner friendly: Left justify the entire document. Use a sans-serif font, size 10 or higher. Avoid italics, underlining, parentheses, brackets, graphics, and lines.

Internet: Create a text version of your resumé to submit via email or webpage. Make it computer friendly: avoid tabs and unnecessary hard returns. To get flagged by filters, use keywords more than you would on a paper resumé. Example: Developed CRM ERP and SFA applications using C++ Java and SQL for systems using Apache iPlanet and Oracle running on Solaris Linux and Windows.

FORMS: MEMO

Take-away:

Write memos to be read quickly and to be archived for years.

Notes:

"The horror of that moment," the King went on, "I shall never never forget!"
"You will, though," the Queen said, "if you don't make a memorandum of it."

Lewis Carroll

The memo is similar to a letter except that it is used to correspond with people inside the organization. Memos are used to announce, request, confirm, instruct, and inform. But what the memo also does is record: it very often becomes a part of the official archives of the organization. The word *memorandum* comes from the Latin word *memorandus*, which means *to be remembered*. Because it's so easy to create and distribute memos, they often proliferate to the point of absurdity. Many of them would not survive the Embarrassment Test: "Would I really want people to be able to read this five years from now?"

One way to write an effective memo is to imagine that it will be posted on the wall at the entrance to the cafeteria. To entice people to read your memo as they walk by, follow these guidelines:

Tone: Use a positive tone, especially in the subject line.

Subject: Avoid acronyms, dates, and initials.

Reason: Explicitly state the purpose of the memo.

Parallels: Present related statements in bulleted or numbered lists, ideally in brief imperatives.

Focus: Deal only with the subject specified; that is, avoid introducing new topics.

Closing: Tell the readers what you want them to do, even if this is just a restatement of the purpose.

For the memo below, follow the guidelines to make improvements.

To: All Employees	From: Don Chaffin
Subject: HR Summer 2002 Warning by D.C.	Date: May 6, 2002

Employees who spend more than three hours per day in front of a computer monitor may experience eye strain and headaches. This hazard can be avoided by taking three simple actions.
Documents should be placed at the same distance from you as the monitor. Position the monitor perpendicular to and slightly below your line of sight. It helps to take a break every ten minutes, looking far away and making sure to blink.
We in HR will publish the next summer warning, about lower back pain, in 2 weeks.

Subject: ______________________________

____

- ______________________________________
- ______________________________________
- ______________________________________

____

Don't you think your version would do a better job of enticing readers standing in line at the cafeteria? The best memos—the ones most likely to be read—are concise, ideally not longer than one page.

FORMS: REPORT

Take-away:

Early careful thinking is the key to easy report writing.

Notes:

Good writing is clear thinking made visible.

Bill Wheeler

The biggest problem with reports has little to do with grammar or clarity. The biggest problem is bad structure due to a lack of early thinking and planning. Yes, outlining. But outlining does not have to be drudgery. It can be fun, and it can even make the actual writing much easier.

Try the unique approach to outlining used by top-tier business analysts. It has only three rules:

Ideas: Use ideas, not topics, and write them as brief assertive sentences.
Pyramid: Arrange your ideas in a pyramid, topped by your main idea.
Unity: Rewrite each idea so that it summarizes the ideas below it and links to the idea beside it.

Example:

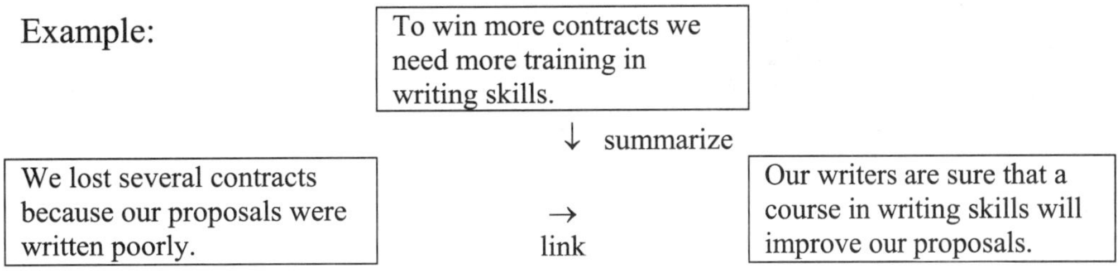

Using these rules, identify which two ideas should be switched in the pyramid below.

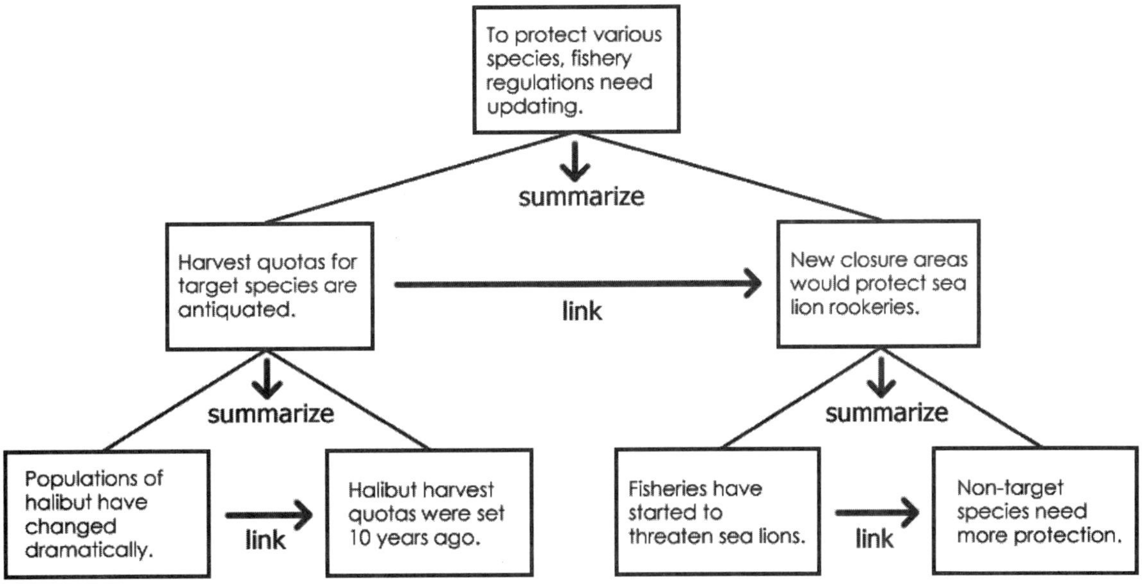

The benefits of using a pyramid to outline include:

1. The main idea will be absolutely clear to you and to the reader.
2. The rewriting of linked ideas improves logical flow.
3. The juggling of ideas enhances creativity.
4. Section headings will jump out at you.
5. Writing can commence anywhere.

Note: The pyramid outline is more suited to reports written to persuade than to reports written merely to inform.

FORMS: PRESENTATION

Take-away:

The best presentation slide is a skimpy outline designed to guide a conversation.

Notes:

Use one chart in a presentation and it will receive 100 percent of the audience's attention; use 100, and none will be memorable.

Gene Zelazny

Use these guidelines to fix the presentation slide below:

Headline: Use active voice. Write no more than one sentence. Use no more than two lines.

Bullets: Use parallel construction at each level. Put main point first, then supporting data. Never write a whole paragraph.

Graphic: Support the headline. Match the text. Choose well →

Fonts: Consistently use a limited set, never smaller than 12pt.

what you want to show	which to use
contribution of components	
differences among items	
change over time	
distribution of occurrence	
correlation between variables	

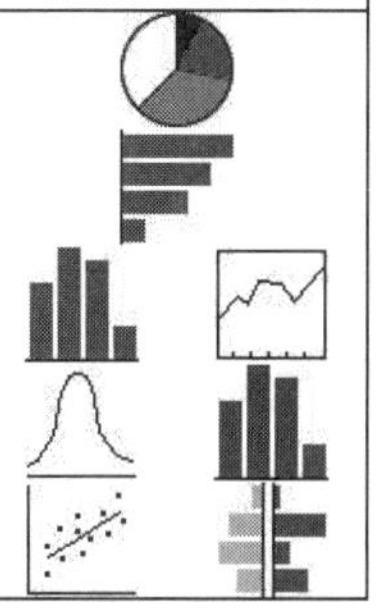

Kicker box: Use sparingly, and only to show why the audience should care about the headline. Never use to show off with impressive facts. Remember: white space is your friend.

The highest proportion of revenues was generated by Project B. Changes among projects were as expected.

- It is expected that Project A will soon expire. This will free up staff for other projects.
- **Project B doubled in size to produce 60% of revenues.**
- Project C contribution remained at 30% of revenues.
- Generation of revenues continues to change among projects.

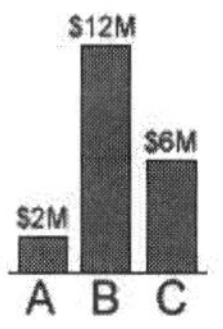

Despite its level share of revenues, Project C sold a record number of units last quarter.

Project Revenues

Every presentation should use the sequence: "Here is what I am going to tell you. Here it is. Here is what I told you." This rule is trite but useful: people remember things better if they hear them three times.

SUMMARY

Bob and Ben appreciate your diligence. They are confident that you will soon be receiving kudos for your writing at work.

Notes:

We covered the writing process from beginning to end in a logical progression:

THINK -	thinking about what we will write
WRITE -	organizing and drafting
EDIT -	editing to make our writing easy to read
USAGE -	editing to make things correct
STYLE -	editing to make things clear and appropriate
FORMS -	editing typical problems in common written formats at work

Note the repetition of the word *editing*. Writing is editing, and good writing only comes from careful editing. Anyone who tells you different is trying to sell you something.

It sounds like a lot of work, doesn't it? Well it does require extra work as you develop your skills in editing. But it gets much easier after those skills are mastered.

These writing and editing skills are life skills: the better you write, the better you think. The benefits spill over into all aspects of your life, at work and at home.

I don't know any but the simplest rules of English grammar, and I seldom consciously apply them. Nevertheless, I instinctively write correctly and, I like to think, in an interesting fashion. I know when something sounds right and when it doesn't, and I can tell the difference without hesitation, even when writing at breakneck speed. How do I do this? I haven't the faintest idea.

Isaac Asimov

THINK	AFFIRM	Bad writing is everywhere. We are all part of the problem: we tolerate it every day.
	DECIDE	Sometimes it's better *not* to put something in writing.
	DEFINE	Make it a habit to write a purpose any time you write a subject.
	DESCRIBE	Describe your reader reading: use words if that's how you visualize best.
	DEPICT	Describe your reader reading: use images if that's how you visualize best.
	BRAINSTORM	To jumpstart your writing, brainstorm with clustering.
WRITE	OPEN	Open documents with a brief introduction to the nature, issues, and findings.
	PERSUADE	Think early about how you will order your ideas to best persuade your reader.
	ORGANIZE	Organize early—be a diplomat and be a director.
	OUTLINE	The best outline is a flexible list of brief statements that support your purpose.
	DRAFT	Write the draft fast, expecting that it will be a mess in need of editing.
	REST	After the draft, take a break from writing; the creative work will continue.
EDIT	JUDGE	Rules help us to understand each other, but they do not guarantee it.
	CLARIFY	Ponderous writing is a habit in many professions, but it's a habit you can change.
	ALIGN	Reading is easier when the grammar aligns with the story.
	GUIDE	Readers like to be guided with transitions and links.
	VARY	Keep readers interested: vary sentence length and format.
	ENGAGE	Use hooks to repeatedly engage your reader.
	PROOFREAD	Proofreading is best done on paper and by a friend.
USAGE	APOSTROPHE	To remember how to use the apostrophe, use a mnemonic device.
	COMMA	Readers are guided by commas, so use them liberally but carefully.
	HOMONYM	Create silly memory aids, and you won't have to look up homonyms forever.
	VERB	Make editing a speed-reading game to find mismatches between subject and verb.
	PRONOUN	Every pronoun reference should be obvious, correct, and consistent.
	MODIFIER	Avoid making your readers have to interpret or move your modifiers.
	PARALLEL	Prose without parallels is music without rhythm: easy to create, but hard to enjoy.
STYLE	PASSIVITY	Passive voice numbs the mind of the reader: avoid it when you can.
	WORDINESS	Avoid wordiness.
	IMPRECISION	Keep readers interested by using lively verbs, unique nouns, and details.
	NEGATIVITY	Make positives out of negatives so that readers pay attention and understand.
	DRIVEL	Clichés, legalese, and buzzwords are okay, but only if used in moderation.
	VANITY	Readers pay better attention if you use the word *you* more than you use *I* or *we*.
	BIAS	Sensitivity to bias is essential to writers who want to continue to be read.
FORMS	EMAIL	Write and send emails with the same care that you write and send letters.
	LETTER	The best letters use simple words, full thoughts, and assertive endings.
	RESUMÉ	Fill your resumé with active descriptions of capabilities and accomplishments.
	MEMO	Write memos to be read quickly and to be archived for years.
	REPORT	Early careful thinking is the key to easy report writing.
	PRESENTATION	The best presentation slide is a skimpy outline designed to guide a conversation.

Everyone should have a dictionary and a thesaurus at their desk.

After that, the most useful resource to have is *The Gregg Reference Manual*. You will have fun using it to settle arguments with colleagues about proper usage.

The author, William Sabin, is a retired publisher of business books. He has written many articles in the area of language and communication, and he speaks frequently at conferences.

If you are an okay writer and you want to be a good writer, get *The Elements of Style*. It has become almost a cliché to recommend this book. The reason is that it is that good. And it's short, too.

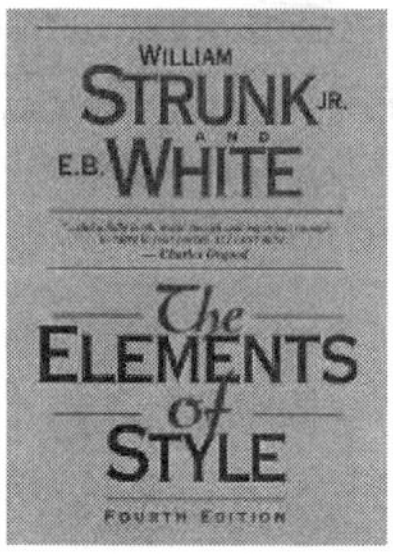

The original author, William Strunk, was a teacher of English at Cornell in the early 1900s.

The revising author, E. B. White, was an essayist, a poet, and an author of children's books including *Charlotte's Web* and *Stuart Little*.

If you are a good writer and you want to be a very good writer, get *Style: Ten Lessons in Clarity and Grace.* This book is not just about style. It explains why bad writing is bad and good writing is good. It shows you how to edit a draft and turn it into a polished work of clarity, coherence, and personality.

The author, Joseph Williams, is a Professor Emeritus of English at the University of Chicago.

Other useful references:

Writing for Results by David Ewing
Written by a Harvard professor. Unfortunately now out of print. You will have to get a used copy somewhere. This book has excellent sections on persuasion and on writing for publication.

The Plain English Guide by Martin Cutts
Written by a British consultant. We found this gem in London. Good luck finding a copy, but congratulations if you do. It emphasizes how to write clearly for your customers.

Essential English Grammar by Philip Gucker
An inexpensive self-study workbook that thoroughly reviews grammar, for writing and for speaking. It has more than 600 practice exercises with solutions.

> I must say I find television very educational. The minute somebody turns it on, I go to the library and read a good book.
>
> *Groucho Marx*

1. Similar things should be coordinated by writing them in: (A) deadwood (B) parallel (C) context (D) format	1. ⒶⒷⒸⒹ
2. Symptoms of _____ include deadwood, bloat, and buried verbs. (A) imprecision (B) drivel (C) vanity (D) wordiness	2. ⒶⒷⒸⒹ
3. Two types of transitions that guide the reader are: (A) amplify, emphasize (B) jargon, bias (C) distance, separate (D) font, color	3. ⒶⒷⒸⒹ
4. Use passive voice when the doer is: (A) unknown (B) unimportant (C) confidential (D) A, B, or C	4. ⒶⒷⒸⒹ
5. Clear writing is achieved when we _____ the grammar with the story. (A) align (B) format (C) vary (D) guide	5. ⒶⒷⒸⒹ
6. The drivel of clichés, legalese, and buzzwords is bad when used in: (A) moderation (B) memos (C) excess (D) email	6. ⒶⒷⒸⒹ
7. To keep readers interested, vary: (A) draft regimen (B) template structure (C) hackneyed phrases (D) sentence length	7. ⒶⒷⒸⒹ
8. To continually engage the reader, use: (A) commas (B) hooks (C) drivel (D) A and B	8. ⒶⒷⒸⒹ
9. Bland qualifiers and generic nouns are examples of: (A) negativity (B) bias (C) imprecision (D) passivity	9. ⒶⒷⒸⒹ
10. *Ben wrote an email to Bob about his tardiness.* What is the pronoun problem? (A) shift (B) squinting (C) limbo (D) mismatch	10. ⒶⒷⒸⒹ
11. *With regard to our telecon yesterday.* In letters, avoid this kind of: (A) informal beginning (B) insincere politeness (C) half thought (D) imperative tone	11. ⒶⒷⒸⒹ
12. Which should use a verb? (A) subject (B) purpose (C) topic (D) link	12. ⒶⒷⒸⒹ
13. Two independent clauses joined by a conjunction also need a: (A) homonym (B) hook (C) comma (D) modifier	13. ⒶⒷⒸⒹ
14. *Ben recalled clearly warning Bob.* The modifier is: (A) misplaced (B) squinting (C) disruptive (D) dangling	14. ⒶⒷⒸⒹ
15. What should be given veto power over a standard format for an outline? (A) chronology (B) template (C) guide (D) purpose	15. ⒶⒷⒸⒹ
16. To avoid sending imperfect emails, what should be typed first? (A) From: (B) To: (C) Subject: (D) Message:	16. ⒶⒷⒸⒹ
17. *Its owner said, "Its voice is its own."* How many apostrophes should be added? (A) none (B) one (C) two (D) three	17. ⒶⒷⒸⒹ
18. To comprehend a negative, people first imagine the positive and then: (A) cancel it (B) extract it (C) depict it (D) splice it	18. ⒶⒷⒸⒹ
19. When used as a verb, the word *affect* does not mean: (A) influence (B) pretend (C) persuade (D) cause	19. ⒶⒷⒸⒹ
20. The essential components of an opening are _____, issues, and findings. (A) sequence (B) nature (C) format (D) tact	20. ⒶⒷⒸⒹ

Note: Check your answers by folding this page back a bit and comparing your selections to those on page 91.

Still haven't had enough?

Here are some extra credit questions:

A. The ideas you explain in detail in the middle of a piece of writing have a better chance of being remembered than do the ideas you present first and last.

True or False?

B. Besides rules and opinions, the other source of authority in writing is grammar.

True or False?

C. In a presentation slide, a headline with two sentences, even if written in passive voice, is a good way to signal the importance of an issue.

True or False?

A. The idea presented first has primacy; the idea presented last has recency. The ideas you state first and last have a better chance of being remembered than do the ideas placed in the middle. The answer is: False. [see the lesson: Persuade]

B. The third source of authority in writing is usage. By this we mean how most people generally use English. The answer is: False. [see the lesson: Judge]

C. Brevity is power in a presentation slide. For the headline of a slide: Use active voice. Write no more than one sentence. Use no more than two lines. The answer is: False. [see the lesson: Presentation]

1. Similar things should be coordinated by writing them in: (A) deadwood (B) parallel (C) context (D) format	1. Ⓐ●ⒸⒹ
2. Symptoms of _____ include deadwood, bloat, and buried verbs. (A) imprecision (B) drivel (C) vanity (D) wordiness	2. ⒶⒷⒸ●
3. Two types of transitions that guide the reader are: (A) amplify, emphasize (B) jargon, bias (C) distance, separate (D) font, color	3. ●ⒷⒸⒹ
4. Use passive voice when the doer is: (A) unknown (B) unimportant (C) confidential (D) A, B, or C	4. ⒶⒷⒸ●
5. Clear writing is achieved when we _____ the grammar with the story. (A) align (B) format (C) vary (D) guide	5. ●ⒷⒸⒹ
6. The drivel of clichés, legalese, and buzzwords is bad when used in: (A) moderation (B) memos (C) excess (D) email	6. ⒶⒷ●Ⓓ
7. To keep readers interested, vary: (A) draft regimen (B) template structure (C) hackneyed phrases (D) sentence length	7. ⒶⒷⒸ●
8. To continually engage the reader, use: (A) commas (B) hooks (C) drivel (D) A and B	8. Ⓐ●ⒸⒹ
9. Bland qualifiers and generic nouns are examples of: (A) negativity (B) bias (C) imprecision (D) passivity	9. ⒶⒷ●Ⓓ
10. *Ben wrote an email to Bob about his tardiness.* What is the pronoun problem? (A) shift (B) squinting (C) limbo (D) mismatch	10. ⒶⒷ●Ⓓ
11. *With regard to our telecon yesterday.* In letters, avoid this kind of: (A) informal beginning (B) insincere politeness (C) half thought (D) imperative tone	11. ⒶⒷ●Ⓓ
12. Which should use a verb? (A) subject (B) purpose (C) topic (D) link	12. Ⓐ●ⒸⒹ
13. Two independent clauses joined by a conjunction also need a: (A) homonym (B) hook (C) comma (D) modifier	13. ⒶⒷ●Ⓓ
14. *Ben recalled clearly warning Bob.* The modifier is: (A) misplaced (B) squinting (C) disruptive (D) dangling	14. Ⓐ●ⒸⒹ
15. What should be given veto power over a standard format for an outline? (A) chronology (B) template (C) guide (D) purpose	15. ⒶⒷⒸ●
16. To avoid sending imperfect emails, what should be typed first? (A) From: (B) To: (C) Subject: (D) Message:	16. ⒶⒷⒸ●
17. *Its owner said, "Its voice is its own."* How many apostrophes should be added? (A) none (B) one (C) two (D) three	17. ●ⒷⒸⒹ
18. To comprehend a negative, people first imagine the positive and then: (A) cancel it (B) extract it (C) depict it (D) splice it	18. ●ⒷⒸⒹ
19. When used as a verb, the word *affect* does not mean: (A) influence (B) pretend (C) persuade (D) cause	19. ⒶⒷⒸ●
20. The essential components of an opening are _____, issues, and findings. (A) sequence (B) nature (C) format (D) tact	20. Ⓐ●ⒸⒹ

The life so short, the craft so long to learn. *Geoffrey Chaucer*

AFFIRM
(E) All of the above.

OPEN
fallacy: 3. Readers will want to experience it in the same sequence that I did.
component: findings

PERSUADE
· I come to bury Caesar, not to praise him (primacy message: **Relax, I am here to mourn, too.**)
· The evil that men do lives after them
· Brutus says he was ambitious
· Brutus is an honorable man
· You all did love him once, not without cause
· O judgment, thou art fled to brutish beasts (recency message: **Brutus is a beast!**)

Sides: Be **political**.
Facts: Be **selective**.
Problems: Be **sensitive**.
Testimonials: Be **credible**.
Recommendations: Be **decisive**.
Hyperbole: Be **restrained**.

ORGANIZE
sort: 1,3,5,9 → A 4,6,11,12 → B 2,7,8,10 → C
order: B → C → A (When asking for something, give reasons before requests.)

OUTLINE
irrelevant: I, II

- Protect against a virus
  - **Employees should take responsibility**
    - Use a virus-scanning program
    - Block executable code
    - Make regular backups
  - **Departments should educate and audit**
    - Distribute security bulletins
    - Audit anti-virus software
- Follow emergency procedures
  - Isolate your computer
  - Call the hotline

REST
1-D: poem *Kublai Kan* dreamed by Coleridge
2-A: periodic table dreamed by Mendeleyev
3-E: induction motor daydreamed by Tesla
4-C: manufacture of insulin dreamed by Banting
5-B: song *Yesterday* dreamed by McCartney
6-F: gene chip daydreamed by Brown

JUDGE
Red is a color in America but a colour in Canada. New words are not in old dictionaries.
Strict adherence to rules of grammar (never end a sentence with a preposition) can make us sound silly.
There are too many exceptions. If we replace "microscopic" with "tiny" our writing becomes less precise.

CLARIFY

1. It explains how to **organize similar factories**.
2. It explains how to **compete well repeatedly**.

ALIGN

actor: **consultant** action: **understands** actor: **managers** action: **argued**

Our **consultant understands** that **managers argued** frequently.

GUIDE

Collection-type heritage assets acquired in fiscal 2000 amounted to $61 million. The public entrusts the government with **them** and holds it accountable for their preservation.

These assets are preserved in three places. The Library of Congress holds the world's largest library collection: 115 million items. **Also,** the Smithsonian Institution holds 140 million objects for public exhibition. **In addition,** the National Archives holds 2 million cubic feet of records, including the U.S. Constitution. [alternatively: **First,** the Library of Congress ... **Second,** the S ... **Third,** the N ...]

VARY

With a detailed survey, we were able to find out what people thought about the cafeteria. **The results were not surprising.** The menu was considered**—by every single respondent—**to be monotonous to the point of torture. Cafeteria managers were finally able to learn the key to pleasing their customers**:** **variety**.

ENGAGE (some possibilities—be creative)

definition:	**AAR - a candid forum with decorum**
prediction:	**Truth will be revealed at the AAR.**
question:	**After an AAR, will we walk the talk?**
joke:	**Talk, learn, improve: be AAR that you can be.**

Soliciting reader response:

Contact me with any questions.

PROOFREAD

I need **your advice**. **You're** my "guru of goop**."** **There may be** trouble with the mixture. **Shouldn't** we package it in plastic**?** **It's** like mashed **potatoes**. It will travel by **plane**, **then** by train.

This work **environment** is like a race **course**: it's frantic and loud. Wouldn't you like some **peace and** quiet**?** This **week** we **shouldn't** be **here**. But a **break** from the action might be **too** much to ask **for**.

APOSTROPHE

It's an odd parrot that mimics its own voice.

COMMA

1. compound sentence:	Nikola Tesla invented the induction **motor, but** electric resonance was his passion.
2. series separator:	Charles Steinmetz expanded our knowledge in hysteresis, **modeling, and** lightning.
3. introductory element:	Discovered by Michael **Faraday, electromagnetic** induction electrified the world.
4. comma splice:	Thomas Edison tried his **best, but** his direct-current systems lost out.

HOMONYM

The acquisition will **complement** our product line and please our **principal** investor, but it will also adversely **affect** morale.

Some managers were **averse** to our plan to **ensure** that we would have **continual** performance reviews.

VERB

Everyone in the organization, including my colleagues, **understands** that we want to maintain a learning culture. We believe that it is appropriate for humans to be proactive problem solvers. **Each** reality and truth about our working environment **is** pragmatically discovered. Accurate **data and** relevant **information flow** freely in a fully-connected network. **Human nature**, though presumed good for most people, **is** at least mutable. My **group** in Marketing and Sales **believes** that diverse but connected units are good for the organization. We also believe that we must allow for a diversity of task-oriented and relationship-orientated people.

PRONOUN

1. mismatch: The consultants presented a detailed briefing about how **they** could help the client.
2. limbo: After talking with the attorney, my **boss modified her** presentation.
3. shift: I liked the creative maneuvering, the competition gunning for **me**, and the feeling that I was in a race to dominate the field.

MODIFIER (some suggestions)

1. disruptive: The electricity was unavailable for several hours **because the utility company was having trouble meeting peak demand**.
2. misplaced: **At a meeting yesterday**, the accountant said she will need all departments to submit their budgets to her office.
3. dangling: **His mentor** told stories about the early days of the company.
4. squinting: Programmers who **repeatedly** change code frustrate our project managers.

PARALLEL

The committee recommends spending the surplus on an office party and **increasing** next year's budget for entertainment expenses.

Anyone requesting a change from last year's budget should follow proper procedures:

- **Use only the standard form.**
- Include a detailed description.
- **Submit your request by Tuesday.**

The auditor discovered mistakes in accounts receivable, found receipts that had not been recorded, and corrected several ledger **entries. All this time** our accountant could not be found.

PASSIVITY

Ben isolated a problem with the server.
The access logs identified the source of the problem.
Ben announced that the server had crashed.

WORDINESS

~~This letter is to advise you that~~ your office is ~~in the process of~~ being cleaned; ~~it should also be noted that~~ extra work is required ~~to be carried out~~ on the carpets and drapes.
To **finish** the project, you will need **money** for **emergencies**.
We **suspect** that if you **recommend** leniency, they will **conclude** that our plan is not to **object**.

IMPRECISION

~~Pretty~~ soon we should be ~~very~~ alert to the ~~rather~~ odd way it gets ~~a little~~ worse.
A penny saved is **a penny** earned.
Each week, 3 million affluent business travelers read *The Economist*.

SOLUTIONS TO THE LESSONS

NEGATIVITY

We demand that you cease complaining that the alleged problem was our fault.
Please work with us to investigate and explain the incident.
Managers **may ask for increased budgets if they spent more than 90% of last year's money**.

DRIVEL

clichés: **We will be in trouble if we don't start over, work hard, and get it finished.**
legalese: **Here is the appendix.**
buzzwords: **(This person is annoying and afraid of being fired.)**

VANITY

You are invited to a seminar about our services.
Your time is valuable, so we streamlined our presentation.
And please do call with any questions; we would be happy to talk with you.

BIAS

Edith and Woodrow Wilson agreed: the **average person** would be better off if **representatives** voted **their** conscience about the 19th amendment.
Our nurse will meet with **the lawyer** and **the engineer**.

EMAIL

Subject: **Email and the virus**
Our system crashed because of the virus attached to the email you inadvertently broadcast.
To make sure this does not happen again:
(1) Please turn on your virus-checking program.
(2) Avoid using the Reply To All button when responding to email.

LETTER

Dear Academy:
I am writing about the movie, *Evolution*, directed by Ivan Reitman.
Please ensure that the Academy gives careful consideration to **the movie**. Despite the unabashed product placement, it is a well-acted romantic action comedy.
I will deliver a DVD of the movie to your office on 12 December.
Respectfully,

RESUMÉ

EXPERIENCE
Training Coordinator, St. Mary's College, San Antonio, Texas 1996 - 2002

- Enrolled employees in training classes and prepared facilities for presentations.
- **Developed** a new class in conflict resolution ~~was set up~~ for department administrators. [action verb]
- ~~Employee participation in training classes varied with staff size.~~ [not a capability or accomplishment]

Assistant Manager, Barnes & Noble Bookstore, San Antonio, Texas 1992 - 1996

- **Managed** inventory for books, music CDs, calendars, and magazines. [incomplete sentence preferred]
- **Led** book discussion groups and arranged author events. [spelling]

EDUCATION
Diploma, San Houston High School, San Antonio, Texas 1992
ACTIVITIES
Train tutors for Literacy Volunteers
~~Religious Advisor, Hash House Harriers of San Antonio~~ [irrelevant association]

MEMO

Subject: **Protect Your Eyes**

The purpose of this memo is to give you simple actions you can take to protect your eyes if you spend more than three hours per day in front of a computer monitor.

1. **Place documents at the same distance from you as the monitor.**
2. Position the monitor perpendicular to and slightly below your line of sight.
3. **Take a break every ten minutes, looking far away and making sure to blink.**

Try these actions to avoid eye strain and headaches, and please suggest the same to your co-workers.

REPORT

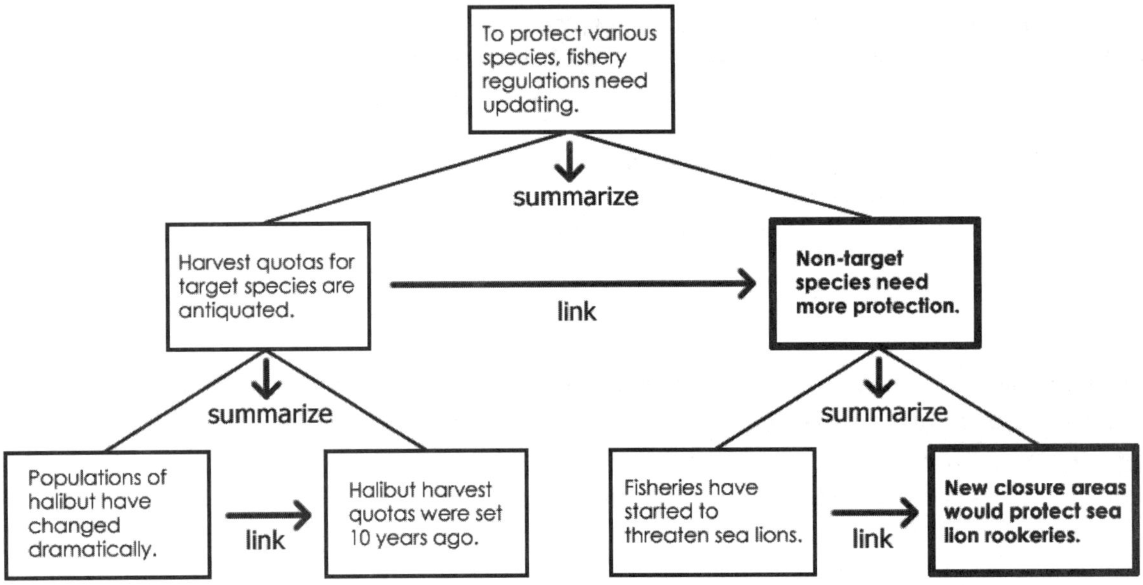

PRESENTATION

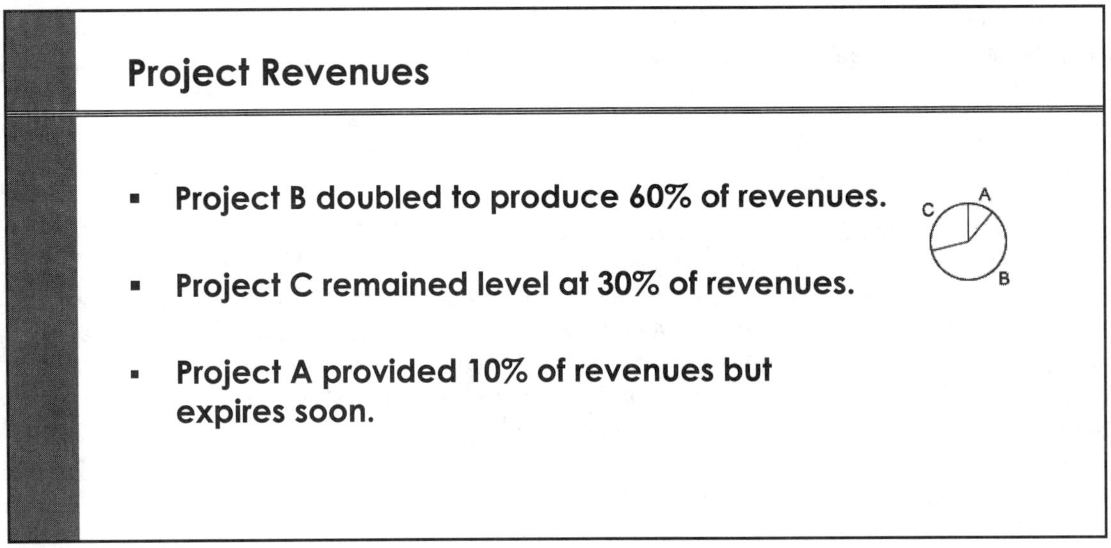

Part 2

Practice

LESSONS	28 EXERCISES	Repeat the lessons to learn them well.
CLARITY	140 EXERCISES	Avoid distracting the reader. Watch for unnecessary words, redundant phrases, and fuzzy verbs.
IDIOM	36 EXERCISES	Learn the customs for the correct use of certain prepositions and grammatical constructions.
WORDS	100 EXERCISES	Improve your business vocabulary by guessing and checking.

Practice makes perfect, especially with writing. Here is a full set of exercises for you to practice the concepts in this workbook. Solutions are on the following page.

OPEN

Rewrite the opening to the declaration of Independence. Use one brief sentence for each of the three components (nature, issues, findings). Don't worry about how Thomas Jefferson wrote it; write your own clear and assertive version.

When in the Course of human events, it becomes necessary for one people to dissolve the political bands which have connected them with another, and to assume among the powers of the earth, the separate and equal station to which the Laws of Nature and of Nature's God entitle them, a decent respect to the opinions of mankind requires that they should declare the causes which impel them to the separation.

PERSUADE

King Lear summons his three daughters and asks them how much they each love him. They know their answers will influence how he bequeaths his estate. His loyal adviser, the Earl of Kent, beseeches Lear to recognize that his youngest, and favorite, daughter Cordelia is being truthful, and is showing fortitude by not stooping as low as her two sisters, who are lying to get rich. King Lear is livid at the impertinence of the Earl of Kent and remains resolutely unpersuaded (hence the tragedy).

Here are some lines by the Earl of Kent:

- Royal Lear, whom I have ever honour'd — primacy message: I serve only you.
- Cheque this hideous rashness
- Thy youngest daughter does not love thee least
- See better, Lear; and let me still remain
- I'll tell thee thou dost evil — recency message: You are wrong!

Note that the speaker is dealing with a hostile audience and has obviously chosen sides. Remember the format advice for persuading when taking sides: for a hostile audience, always present both sides. Now, try to do a better job of convincing King Lear: say things nicer in line 2, show both sides in line 4, and finally, in line 5 write a recency message that will tug at the heartstrings of the cantankerous king.

The Earl of Kent, toned down and formatted to persuade:

1 • Royal Lear, whom I have ever honour'd — primacy message: I serve only you.

2 • ______________________________

3 • Thy youngest daughter does not love thee least

4 • ______________________________

5 • ______________________________ — recency message: She is like you.

OPEN

Note that Thomas Jefferson did not declare independence in his opening. He wrote that if one *were* to separate from another, it is appropriate to explain why. We are much more direct—some would say blunt—in the solution we present below.

This document declares our independence. (findings)
We felt it necessary to give the reasons for our decision. (nature)
Our 37 grievances against the tyrant are listed below. (issues)

With this solution we are suggesting that the order of the components is not as important as the presence of all three components. Whether this replacement opening is good, or whether yours is good, is obviously a subjective issue.

Comment: Thomas Jefferson wrote his opening paragraph to speak not only to the king, but to the leaders and citizens of Great Britain. Jumping one lesson ahead to Persuade, we could say that his opening, while explaining the *nature* of the document, conveys a *primacy* message of, "We are like you—civilized and deserving of being politically equal—so let us tell you why we are suggesting a separation." After 37 paragraphs of grievances, or *issues*, he finally presents in the final paragraph his *findings* via his *recency* message, "We declare that these United Colonies are Free and Independent States."

PERSUADE

The Earl of Kent, toned down and formatted to persuade:

- Royal Lear, whom I have ever honour'd — primacy message: I serve only you.

- **Please, give this more thought**
- Thy youngest daughter does not love thee least
- **All three love you, but two only flatter**

- **See your proud self in the truthful one** — recency message: She is like you.

ORGANIZE

In the example below, assume the opening will be used. Sort each item in the list by drawing a line to one of groups A, B, or C, which have been given brief titles. Be a diplomat and a director: order the groups.

Opening: Analysis of our controversial transition to all online training shows that we still need classroom training.

Item	No.
users of online courses show low completion rates	1
training effectiveness has degraded	2
managers are too busy to use online courses	3
classroom training had better test scores	4
the main training users are now less committed to training	5
managers were the dominant users of classroom training	6
outside trainers are reluctant to convert to online format	7
our relations with outside trainers is suffering	8
half of classroom courses were designed by outside trainers	9

Group	Title
A	online training
B	training conclusions
C	classroom training

order: ☐ → ☐ → ☐

OUTLINE

For the outline below, assume the subject and purpose are accurate, and make the following changes:

- Delete the unnecessary section.
- Make it look less like a table of contents.
- Replace one-word headings with brief assertive sentences.

Subject: A multicultural organization
(Purpose: Instruct leaders to address diversity.)

1. Leadership
    - 1.1 Make diversity a core value.
    - 1.2 Include managing diversity in our strategy.
    - 1.3 Commit resources for the long-term.
2. Education
    - 2.1 Give workshops about diversity issues.
    - 2.2 Provide introductory as well as advanced training.
    - 2.3 Develop in-house training expertise.
3. Measurement
    - 3.1 Assess equal-opportunity profile data.
    - 3.2 Survey attitudes and perceptions of employees.
    - 3.3 Track differential career experiences.
4. Culture
    - 4.1 Definitions suffer from semantic confusion.
    - 4.2 Views include integration, differentiation, and fragmentation.
    - 4.3 Researchers identify norms, values, rules, and myths.

ORGANIZE

sort: 1,3,7 → A   2,5,8 → B   4,6,9 → C

order: A → C → B or C → A → B (When the topic is contentious, give details before conclusions.)

OUTLINE

Subject: A multicultural organization

- **Address diversity at the highest level.**
  - → Make diversity a core value.
  - → Include managing diversity in our strategy.
  - → Commit resources for the long-term.
- **Train employees to value diversity.**
  - → Give workshops about diversity issues.
  - → Provide introductory as well as advanced training.
  - → Develop in-house training expertise.
- **Collect information about diversity issues.**
  - → Assess equal-opportunity profile data.
  - → Survey attitudes and perceptions of employees.
  - → Track differential career experiences.

ENGAGE

Assume the sentence below summarizes a section in a report. Now assume you need to write a heading for that section. Write pithy hooks that capture some of the essence of the sentence. Try to use fewer than nine words for each one.

Admiral McCain explained that, because Section 15 of the Federal Acquisition Regulation (FAR) allows flexibility for oral proposals that complement written proposals, we may accept oral presentation of information about past performance, in response to a series of questions in the request for proposals.

definition: ______________________________

prediction: ______________________________

quote: "Let them speak about the past," said Admiral McCain.

question: ______________________________

story: The admiral explained that we may listen.

joke: ______________________________

ALIGN

In the following sentence, identify the actors and their actions, then align the grammar to the story.

The decision by the supervisor was that growth of the staff will occur next year.

actor: ____________ action: ____________ actor: ____________ action: ____________

____

ENGAGE (some possibilities—be creative)

Admiral McCain explained that, because Section 15 of the Federal Acquisition Regulation (FAR) allows flexibility for oral proposals that complement written proposals, we may accept oral presentation of information about past performance, in response to a series of questions in the request for proposals.

definition: **FAR - oral proposals may answer questions**

prediction: **If we ask, they may answer—in person.**

quote: "Let them speak about the past," said Admiral McCain.

question: **Can we talk?**

story: The admiral explained that we may listen.

joke: **Speak up! You will be heard from a FAR.**

ALIGN

actor: **supervisor** action: **decided** actor: **staff** action: **will grow**

The **supervisor decided** that the **staff will grow** next year.

GUIDE

In the paragraphs below, improve flow by doing the following:

- Replace a long noun phrase with a pronoun in the first paragraph.
- Insert a linking sentence at the beginning of the second paragraph, repeating the key word *scholars*.
- Insert transitions at the beginning of sentences within the second paragraph, elaborating on the transition sentence.

With a staff of 200 people from 30 countries, the United Nations University spends $36 million each year on research and policy studies by an international community of scholars. The University relies on the international community of scholars for advice and treats them as if they constituted an in-house think-tank.

The Governance Program produces recommendations for current political problems. The Environment Program focuses on sustainable management of natural resources. The Science Program studies the impact of new technologies on developing countries.

VARY

In the paragraph below, add variety to each sentence:

- Start sentence 1 with a prepositional phrase.
- End sentence 2 with a long phrase after a colon.
- Remove half the words (eleven of them) from sentence 4.

Some porcupines rapidly vibrate their tails when alarmed by a snake, producing a peculiar sound by the striking together of hollow quills. The attacker and the attacked use similar means to achieve the goal of making themselves as dreadful as possible to each other. Suppose those best able to frighten away their enemies escape, but those best fitted for killing and devouring survive in larger numbers. Then in the one case as in the other, the beneficial variations would commonly be preserved through the survival of the fittest.

GUIDE

With a staff of 200 people from 30 countries, the United Nations University spends $36 million each year on research and policy studies by an international community of scholars. The University relies on **them** for advice and treats them as if they constituted an in-house think-tank.

These scholars provide advice for a variety of programs. For example, the Governance Program produces recommendations for current political problems. **Also,** the Environment Program focuses on sustainable management of natural resources. **In addition,** the Science Program studies the impact of new technologies on developing countries.

VARY

When alarmed by a snake, some porcupines rapidly vibrate their tails, producing a peculiar sound by the striking together of hollow quills. The attacker and the attacked use similar means **to achieve a common goal: making** themselves as dreadful as possible to each other. Suppose those best able to frighten away their enemies escape, but those best fitted for killing and devouring survive in larger numbers. **Then beneficial variations are preserved through survival of the fittest.**

APOSTROPHE

In sentence below, correct any problems with apostrophes.

"It's an odd font that bends its descenders," said Bob's secretary's friend, "so mind your p's and q's."

COMMA

Among the sentences below, there is one instance of each of the four problems with commas. Fix each problem and then identify what kind of problem it was.

We went offline at midnight but customers did not notice until noon.

1. ☐ introductory element ☐ compound sentence ☐ comma splice ☐ series separator

The call center needs new telephones, computers and lighting.

2. ☐ introductory element ☐ compound sentence ☐ comma splice ☐ series separator

We went online at noon, five customers called immediately.

3. ☐ introductory element ☐ compound sentence ☐ comma splice ☐ series separator

However many calls remain unanswered.

4. ☐ introductory element ☐ compound sentence ☐ comma splice ☐ series separator

HOMONYM

In the sentence below, circle the correct homonyms to use.

The signal jumped between several discreet/discrete voltage levels, but the source was stationary/stationery and didn't affect/effect our conclusions.

APOSTROPHE

"It's an odd font that bends its descenders," said Bob's secretary's friend, "so mind your p's and q's."
[correct as is]

COMMA

We went offline at **midnight, but** customers did not notice until noon.

1. ☐ introductory element ☑ compound sentence ☐ comma splice ☐ series separator

The call center needs new telephones, **computers, and** lighting.

2. ☐ introductory element ☐ compound sentence ☐ comma splice ☑ series separator

We went online at **noon, and five** customers called immediately.

3. ☐ introductory element ☐ compound sentence ☑ comma splice ☐ series separator

However, many calls remain unanswered.

4. ☑ introductory element ☐ compound sentence ☐ comma splice ☐ series separator

HOMONYM

The signal jumped between several **discrete** voltage levels, but the source was **stationary** and didn't **affect** our conclusions.

discreet: prudent discrete: distinct	When we meet, be discreet.
stationery: paper stationary: fixed	Buy paper at the stationer.
affect: influence effect: result (noun) effect: cause (verb)	Air affects aardvarks; eels effect electricity.

VERB

Play the game called Line & Link. Read quickly through the paragraph below, following these rules:

1. When you read a noun that appears to be the subject of the sentence or of a clause, underline it with a single line.
2. When you read a verb that looks like the main action of the sentence or clause, underline it with a double line. For a split second consider whether the verb matches the noun you underlined. If not, quickly circle the verb and move on.

All employees in the organization, including Bob, understands that for a contract to exist there must be an offer, an acceptance, and consideration. An offer is a statement that indicates a willingness to enter into a bargain on the terms stated. Each contract offer proposed by our colleagues are recorded by Ben. Acceptance occurs when the offeree indicates a willingness to accept the bargain proposed by the offeror. Bob and Ben, though normally quick on the uptake like the rest of the staff, often gets confused by the term, offeree. Consideration is anything of value that is exchanged by the parties; it can be money, property, or a promise to do something. Bob's group in external affairs, also known as public relations, often give consideration in the form of cash.

PRONOUN

Among the sentences below, there is one instance of each of the three types of confusing pronouns. Make edits for clarity and then identify each type of problem.

She disliked the office bickering, the need to watch one's back, and the feeling that she was being judged.

1. ☐ limbo ☐ mismatch ☐ shift

Their programmer had a discussion with our engineer that changed his mind about the action plan.

2. ☐ limbo ☐ mismatch ☐ shift

Our accountants wrote a detailed plan about how it could track expenses.

3. ☐ limbo ☐ mismatch ☐ shift

VERB

All employees in the organization, including Bob, **understand** that for a contract to exist there must be an offer, an acceptance, and consideration. An offer is a statement that indicates a willingness to enter into a bargain on the terms stated. Each contract offer proposed by our colleagues **is** recorded by Ben. Acceptance occurs when the offeree indicates a willingness to accept the bargain proposed by the offeror. Bob and Ben, though normally quick on the uptake like the rest of the staff, often **get** confused by the term, offeree. Consideration is anything of value that is exchanged by the parties; it can be money, property, or a promise to do something. Bob's group in external affairs, also known as public relations, often **gives** consideration in the form of cash.

There are seven sentences in the paragraph above. You should have found an error in four of them.

PRONOUN

She disliked the office bickering, the need to watch **her** back, and the feeling that she was being judged.

1. ☐ limbo ☐ mismatch ☑ shift

Some possibilities:

Their programmer had a discussion with our engineer that changed **the programmer's** mind about the action plan.

Their programmer had a discussion with our engineer that changed **the engineer's** mind about the action plan.

Their programmer had a discussion with our engineer**, who** changed his mind about the action plan.

2. ☑ limbo ☐ mismatch ☐ shift

Our accountants wrote a detailed plan about how **they** could track expenses.

3. ☐ limbo ☑ mismatch ☐ shift

MODIFIER

Among the sentences below, there is one instance of each of the four types of troubled modifiers. Make edits for clarity and then identify each type of problem.

Our technicians, because the service had been interrupted for an entire day, had to work overtime.

1. ☐ misplaced ☐ squinting ☐ disruptive ☐ dangling

The young consultant presented the second report wearing jeans.

2. ☐ misplaced ☐ squinting ☐ disruptive ☐ dangling

Despite being written well, my boss talked on and on about how clarity should be the goal of all interoffice correspondence.

3. ☐ misplaced ☐ squinting ☐ disruptive ☐ dangling

Customers who call about the service repeatedly interrupt our technicians.

4. ☐ misplaced ☐ squinting ☐ disruptive ☐ dangling

PARALLEL

In the example below, make the items in the list grammatically parallel. If one element of a list is a complete sentence and it seems to read okay, then all elements should be complete sentences using a similar form. Use active voice. Use imperatives if possible.

The rules of behavior in the park are as follows:

- On arrival, the rangers want you to register.
- Pack out as much as you pack in.
- Only designated areas for camping.
- At night, food is to be locked up.

MODIFIER (some suggestions)

Our technicians had to work overtime **because the service had been interrupted for an entire day.**

1. ☐ misplaced ☐ squinting ☑ disruptive ☐ dangling

The young consultant **wearing jeans** presented the second report.

2. ☑ misplaced ☐ squinting ☐ disruptive ☐ dangling

Despite the fact that my memo was written well, my boss talked on and on about how clarity should be the goal of all interoffice correspondence.

or:

My boss talked on and on about how clarity should be the goal of all interoffice correspondence.

3. ☐ misplaced ☐ squinting ☐ disruptive ☑ dangling

Customers who **repeatedly** call about the service interrupt our technicians.

or:

Customers who call about the service **are repeatedly interrupting** our technicians.

4. ☐ misplaced ☑ squinting ☐ disruptive ☐ dangling

PARALLEL

The rules of behavior in the park are as follows:

- **Register with the rangers on arrival.**
- Pack out as much as you pack in.
- **Camp only in designated areas.**
- **Lock up food at night.**

PASSIVITY

For the sentences below, change passive voice to active voice.

transpose the subject:

Rationalization of expenditures for office supplies by administrators is necessary to cut costs.

---

extract the subject:

Within the cabinet a paucity of supplies was revealed.

---

supply the subject:

It will be explained how the office will continue to function.

WORDINESS

Remove the wordiness from the sentences below.

delete deadwood:

I should mention that in order to change our contract it is a fact that you need both signatures.

---

sandblast bloat:

To establish approval of the contract, it is necessary that you peruse its contents and subsequently administer your signature.

---

uncover buried verbs:

He needed an implementation of a checking account so that he could remit compensation for his utilization of our program that enables interactions with the network.

PASSIVITY

Administrators must rationalize expenditures for office supplies to cut costs.

The cabinet revealed a paucity of supplies.

She will explain how the office will continue to function.

WORDINESS

~~I should mention that in order~~ to change our contract ~~it is a fact that~~ you need both signatures.

To approve the contract, **read it then sign it**.

He needed **to implement** a checking account so that he could **compensate us when he utilized** our program that **interacts** with the network.

or:

He needed **to start** a checking account so that he could **pay** for his **use** of our program that **interacts** with the network.

IMPRECISION

In the first half of the sentence below, cross out the bland qualifiers. In the second half of the sentence, replace two generic prepositional phrases with something more evocative (and remember Benjamin Franklin).

It was pretty obvious that a rather famous saying was very apropos: early to sleep, early to wake makes a man healthy, wealthy, and wise.

NEGATIVITY

In the sentence below, underline the negative words. Then rewrite the sentence using fewer negations and negative words. Be creative, polite, and encouraging.

Under no circumstances should you not remind Bob to avoid careless mistakes.

DRIVEL

In the sentence below, get rid of the clichés and the legalese.

Please be advised that we are in hot water with regards to the law, and the aforesaid is only the tip of the iceberg.

VANITY

In the sentence below, change the focus from being about you to being for the reader and about the reader.

I have a report about the market success of your software. My briefing about the report will be presented tomorrow in your conference room. I hope you will attend.

BIAS

In the sentence below, remove the examples of gender bias.

According to Ms. Amy Tan and Bob, every salesman should record his man-hours of effort.

IMPRECISION

It was ~~pretty~~ obvious that a ~~rather~~ famous saying was ~~very~~ apropos: early to **bed**, early to **rise** makes a man healthy, wealthy, and wise.

or maybe:

~~It was pretty obvious that~~ a ~~rather~~ famous saying was ~~very~~ apropos: early to **bed**, early to **rise** makes a man healthy, wealthy, and wise.

NEGATIVITY

Under no circumstances should you not remind Bob to avoid careless mistakes.

Always remind Bob to **be careful**.

DRIVEL

We are **in trouble** with the law, and **it is likely to get worse**.

VANITY

You are invited to a briefing tomorrow in your conference room, where I will present a report about the market success of your software.

BIAS

According to **Amy** and Bob, every **salesperson** should record **their work-hours** of effort.

EMAIL

Edit the email below, with the goals of being read, being nice, and being professional.

Subject: VIRUS DOWNLOAD

Message: laziness and stupidity r the leading causes of downloading viruses ;-)
here r some tips for u from bob
pay attention to subject lines and use common sense
always use a recent copy of the approved virus-checking software
read the it bulletins for virus alerts

LETTER

In the letter below, find examples of the typical problem areas and suggest improvements.

Academy of Motion Pictures
8949 Wilshire Boulevard
Beverly Hills, CA 90210

To whom it may concern:

With reference to the movie, *American Pie*, directed by Paul Weitz. It has come to my attention that this slice of Americana did not receive any Oscar nominations. I realize we embraced taboos and pushed the limits of the R rating, but it seems to me that the above-mentioned movie should have been nominated, if only for its honesty and edge. I hope we might discuss this more on the telephone.

Kind regards,

Seann William Scott

EMAIL

Subject: **Tips to avoid virus downloads**

Message: **H**ere **are** some tips for **you** from **B**ob:

- **P**ay attention to subject lines and use common sense.
- **A**lways use a recent copy of the approved virus-checking software.
- **R**ead the **IT** bulletins for virus alerts.

LETTER

Academy of Motion Pictures
8949 Wilshire Boulevard
Beverly Hills, CA 90210

Dear Academy:

I am writing about the movie, *American Pie*, directed by Paul Weitz. **This** slice of Americana did not receive any Oscar nominations. I realize we embraced taboos and pushed the limits of the R rating, but it seems to me that **the movie** should have been nominated, if only for its honesty and edge. **I will call next Thursday afternoon to discuss this matter.**

Respectfully,

Seann William Scott

RESUMÉ

Using the 6 rules, make corrections to the resumé below:

Isabelle Munising
909 Hiawatha Avenue
Chelsea, Michigan 48118
(909) 555-1212
munising909@yahoo.com

EXPERIENCE

Humen Resources Director, Thomson-Shore, Dexter, Michigan 1994 to present
- I managed a staff of 15 and reported progress to VP of operations at weekly meetings.
- Coordinated staff needs including recruiting, training, benefits, and compensation.
- Acheived a company goal of reducing the cost of our insurance plans by 25%.
- Approved salary plans and established employee awards program.

Benefits Administrator, Central Michigan Paper Company, Ada, Michigan 1990 - 1994
- Lead a company-wide review and upgrade of software for benefits management.
- Negotiated contracts for HMOs, PPOs, and life insurance carriers.
- Instrumental in championing process improvements to add value to the company's bottom line.

Human Resources Associate, MeadWestvaco Papers, Escanaba, Michigan 1984 - 1988
- Orientation presentations were put together and given to new hires.
- Completed a company rotation program, with 4-month assignments in payroll, accounting, recruiting, marketing, sales, and purchasing.
- The company grew from 950 to 1250 employees during my tenure.

EDUCATION

BS Psychology, Northern Michigan University 1984
MBA, Human Resources emphasis, University of Michigan 1990

ACTIVITIES

Chairperson, Professional Emphasis Group in Technology, Society for Human Resources Management
Member, Black Alumni Association, University of Michigan Business School
Co-Author: Computer Systems for Benefits Administration, 1995, McGraw-Hill

RESUMÉ

Isabelle Munising
909 Hiawatha Avenue
Chelsea, Michigan 48118
(909) 555-1212
munising909@yahoo.com

EXPERIENCE

Human Resources Director, Thomson-Shore, Dexter, Michigan 1994 to present
[spelling]

- **Managed** a staff of 15 and reported progress to VP of operations at weekly meetings.
  [incomplete sentence preferred]
- Coordinated staff needs including recruiting, training, benefits, and compensation.
- **Achieved** a company goal of reducing the cost of our insurance plans by 25%.
  [spelling]
- Approved salary plans and established employee awards program.

Benefits Administrator, Central Michigan Paper Company, Ada, Michigan 1990 - 1994

- **Led** a company-wide review and upgrade of software for benefits management.
  [spelling]
- Negotiated contracts for HMOs, PPOs, and life insurance carriers.
- ~~Instrumental in championing process improvements to add value to the company's bottom line.~~
  [pompous fluff]

Human Resources Associate, MeadWestvaco Papers, Escanaba, Michigan 1984 - 1988

- **Developed and presented** orientations for new hires.
  [action verbs in active voice]
- Completed a company rotation program, with 4-month assignments in payroll, accounting, recruiting, marketing, sales, and purchasing.
- ~~The company grew from 950 to 1250 employees during my tenure.~~
  [not a capability or accomplishment]

EDUCATION

MBA, Human Resources emphasis, University of Michigan 1990
BS Psychology, Northern Michigan University 1984
[reverse chronological order should always be used in both the EDUCATION and EXPERIENCE sections]

ACTIVITIES

Chairperson, Professional Emphasis Group in Technology, Society for Human Resources Management
~~Member, Black Alumni Association, University of Michigan Business School~~
[irrelevant association and strong hint at irrelevant personal data (race)]
Co-Author: Computer Systems for Benefits Administration, 1995, McGraw-Hill

MEMO

Rewrite the memo below using the guidelines for good memos:

To: Publications Staff	From: Martin Cutts
Subject: Bad Brochures and PDM Ignorance	Date: May 6, 2002

Recent brochures designed by our department have been difficult to read and in some cases simply ugly. Text has not been made easily accessible, mostly due to a lack of clear layout. The following are guidelines:

As a guide to legibility, one should use x-height. Set column width at 50-70 letters and spaces. Line spacing should be made to 1/5 of the type face. The temptation to fill whitespace with type should be resisted. Avoid single words forming the last line of a paragraph.

These and other guidelines from our Publications Design Manual were updated recently, but few people seem to be aware of that fact.

Subject: ____________________

- ____________________
- ____________________
- ____________________
- ____________________
- ____________________

MEMO

Subject: **Good Brochure Layout** [positive tone; no acronyms]

The purpose of this memo is to improve the layout of text in our brochures by giving you the following guidelines: [state the purpose]

- **Use x-height as your guide to legibility.** [text parallels]
- Set column width at 50-70 letters and spaces.
- **Make line spacing 1/5 of the type face.**
- **Resist the temptation to fill whitespace with type.**
- Avoid single words forming the last line of a paragraph.

Use these guidelines and others from our Publications Design Manual to make text more easily accessible to readers of our brochures. [no new topics; tell the readers what you want them to do]

REPORT

On the pyramid of ideas below, identify which two ideas should be switched.

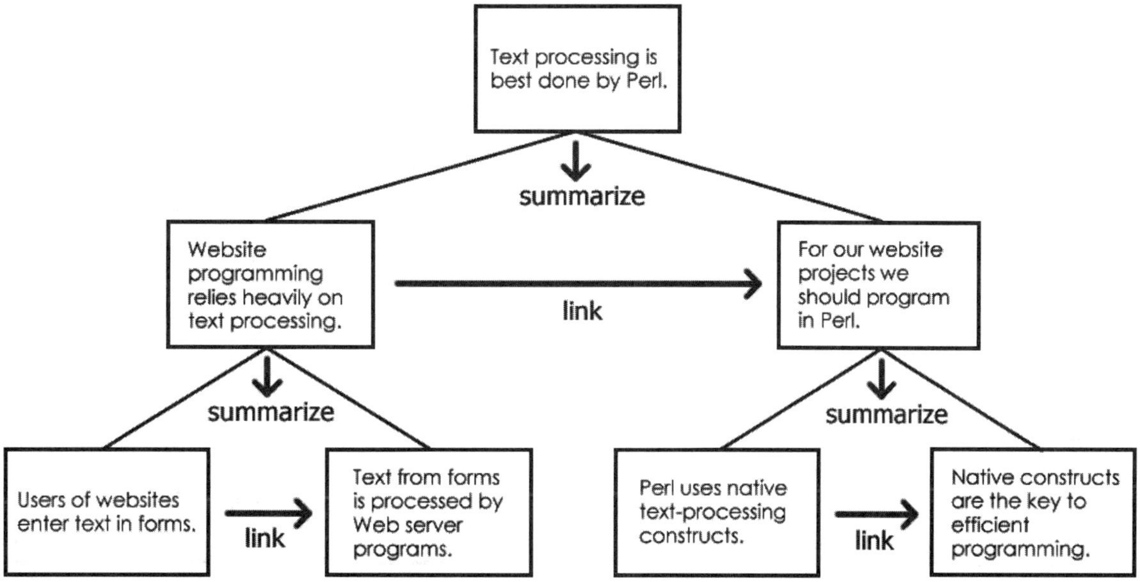

REPORT

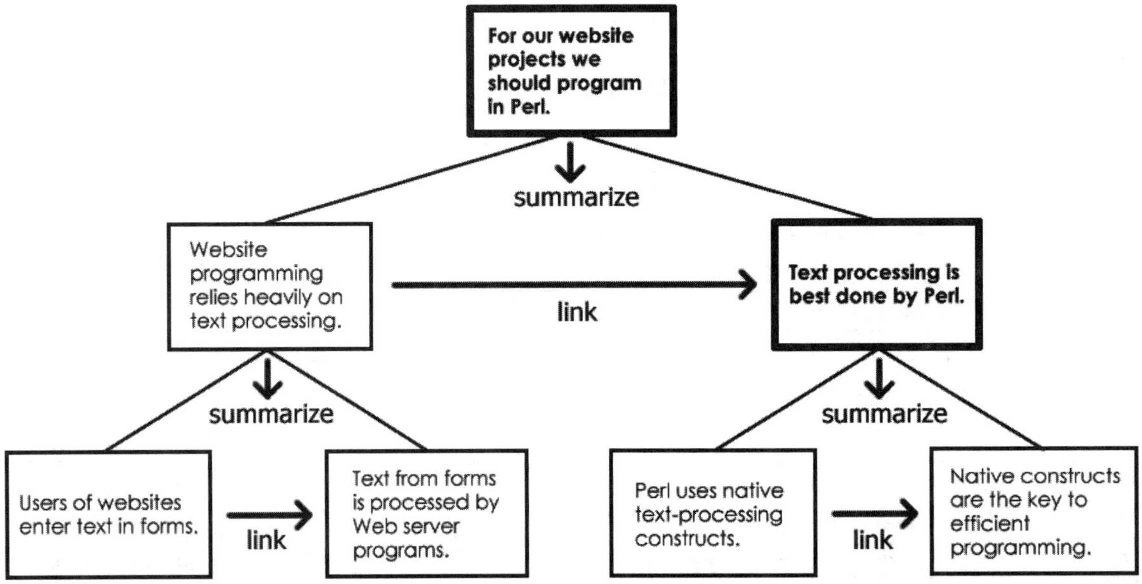
For our website projects we should program in Perl.
summarize
Website programming relies heavily on text processing.
link
Text processing is best done by Perl.
summarize
summarize
Users of websites enter text in forms.
link
Text from forms is processed by Web server programs.
Perl uses native text-processing constructs.
link
Native constructs are the key to efficient programming.

PRESENTATION

Use the presentation guidelines to fix the slide below.

Applications continue to be received. The highest number of applications was received in the third quarter of the year.

- Applications are tracked and reviewed by senior staff.
- **Of the 3Q applications, 40% had unacceptable qualifications.**
- The normal quarterly rate of applications was seen to increase from 24 last year to about 28 this year. (This is most likely due to our increased advertising in the newspaper.)
- Applications are typically even through all four quarters. For the past decade this has been the case. Our surprising 3Q result, twice the normal rate, has yet to be explained.

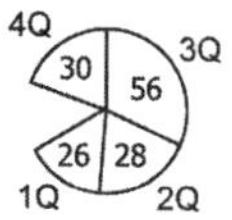

All applicants are benefiting from our new streamlined procedures.

Rising applications spiked during 3Q

PRESENTATION

Rising applications spiked during 3Q

- Applications doubled during 3Q.
  - Cause is unknown
  - 40% lacked qualifications
- The average quarterly rate is rising.
  - From 24 last year to 28 this year
  - Likely due to new advertising

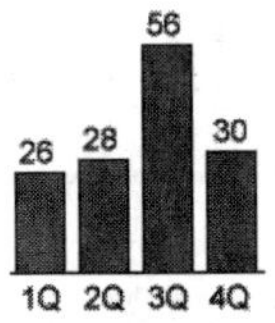

> Man invented language to satisfy his deep need to complain.
>
> *Lily Tomlin*

Unnecessary Words

When we use unnecessary words, we distract or bore the reader. Always strive to remove deadwood, such as the phrase *the purpose of* in the following sentence:

> Government documents are useful for ~~the purpose of~~ showing bad writing at work.

To practice editing for clarity, learn by guessing: cross out unnecessary words and then check your answers on the next page.

1. We should add the point that the 10% estimate does not include losses in productivity.
2. First decide whether you have adequate enough reasons to write the memo.
3. Use the spell checker feature before sending the memo.
4. The memo was improved by means of a well-written purpose.
5. Bob used to think that surrounding circumstances precluded him from writing a purpose.
6. A table describing the reader does not have to be absolutely complete.
7. One necessary condition for good writing is an assessment of the reader.
8. When Bob draws stickpeople, he continues on for hours.
9. Ben thought the cost factor may be prohibitive.
10. Bob wrote about the amount of damage by starting with a mind map.
11. The clusters were drawn in the same way as described in the lesson on brainstorming.
12. Give the elevator speech before they disappear from sight.
13. We had various discussions about the nature, issues, and findings.
14. During the year of 2002, Bob improved his skills in persuasive writing.
15. Ben planned to empty out his file cabinet of testimonials from ex-employees.

Suggested answers:

1. ~~We should add the point that~~ the 10% estimate does not include losses in productivity.
2. First decide whether you have adequate ~~enough~~ reasons to write the memo.
3. Use the spell checker ~~feature~~ before sending the memo.
4. The memo was improved by ~~means of~~ a well-written purpose.
5. Bob used to think that ~~surrounding~~ circumstances precluded him from writing a purpose.
6. A table describing the reader does not have to be ~~absolutely~~ complete.
7. One ~~necessary~~ condition for good writing is an assessment of the reader.
8. When Bob draws stickpeople, he continues ~~on~~ for hours.
9. Ben thought the cost ~~factor~~ may be prohibitive.
10. Bob wrote about the ~~amount of~~ damage by starting with a mind map.
11. The clusters were drawn ~~in the same way~~ as described in the lesson on brainstorming.
12. Give the elevator speech before they disappear ~~from sight~~.
13. We had ~~various~~ discussions about the nature, issues, and findings.
14. During ~~the year of~~ 2002, Bob improved his skills in persuasive writing.
15. Ben planned to empty ~~out~~ his file cabinet of testimonials from ex-employees.

Here are more exercises with unnecessary words:

16. Bob could not successfully escape the need to be a diplomat.

17. His past experience as a director was helpful.

18. Ben's critiques about the outline were few in number but helpful.

19. First and foremost, make it look less like a table of contents.

20. Try not to make the first draft equally as good as a final version.

21. I make sure I have at hand a pencil to record my inspirations.

22. Ben was not physically in the office when he rested.

23. Bob often had his nose inside of a grammar book.

24. Usage is found to be as important as rules or opinions.

25. I should make mention of the lack of clarity in academic writing.

26. To write like a bureaucrat, you should minimize as far as possible the alignment of grammar to story.

27. However, alignment is needed in cases where you want to be clear.

28. The advice about using transitions to guide was duly noted.

29. It is often the case that I forget to use links to guide.

30. Use at least one out of the three ways to vary sentence format.

31. It is my personal opinion that variety in sentence length is the easiest way to keep the reader interested.

32. Bob wrote an engaging hook to introduce the orientation effort planned for the new hires.

33. Few people outside of our department write hooks to keep the reader engaged.

34. Proofreading backwards, Ben passed by several problems with grammar.

35. It's good that Bob will plan ahead to use the apostrophe correctly.

More suggested answers:

16. Bob could not ~~successfully~~ escape the need to be a diplomat.

17. His ~~past~~ experience as a director was helpful.

18. Ben's critiques about the outline were few ~~in number~~ but helpful.

19. First ~~and foremost~~, make it look less like a table of contents.

20. Try not to make the first draft ~~equally~~ as good as a final version.

21. I make sure I have ~~at hand~~ a pencil to record my inspirations.

22. Ben was not ~~physically~~ in the office when he rested.

23. Bob often had his nose inside ~~of~~ a grammar book.

24. Usage is ~~found to be~~ as important as rules or opinions.

25. I should ~~make~~ mention ~~of~~ the lack of clarity in academic writing.

26. To write like a bureaucrat, you should minimize ~~as far as possible~~ the alignment of grammar to story.

27. However, alignment is needed ~~in cases~~ where you want to be clear.

28. The advice about using transitions to guide was ~~duly~~ noted.

29. ~~It is~~ often ~~the case that~~ I forget to use links to guide.

30. Use at least one ~~out~~ of the three ways to vary sentence format.

31. It is my ~~personal~~ opinion that variety in sentence length is the easiest way to keep the reader interested.

32. Bob wrote an engaging hook to introduce the orientation ~~effort~~ planned for the new hires.

33. Few people outside ~~of~~ our department write hooks to keep the reader engaged.

34. Proofreading backwards, Ben passed ~~by~~ several problems with grammar.

35. It's good that Bob will plan ~~ahead~~ to use the apostrophe correctly.

Here are even more exercises with unnecessary words:

36. Ben thinks it's more preferable to put a comma between every pair of elements in a series.

37. All are not averse to the price point of our principal product.

38. The game Line & Link is the one recommended to find mismatches between subject and verb.

39. We will set a new record if all our pronoun references are clear.

40. Writing is not refined in nature if it includes misplaced modifiers.

41. Parallel construction will continue to remain a useful technique.

42. Passive voice and active voice are not one and the same.

43. Passive voice is acceptable in five separate situations.

44. For sentences that are small in size, wordiness is seldom a problem.

45. Learn to delete deadwood so that in the future you will not have a problem with wordiness.

46. It is important to understand the fact that bland qualifiers cause imprecise writing.

47. Describe each new type of thing with precise details.

48. In order to avoid negative reactions, don't use words like *avoid*.

49. The most unique thing about negations is that people first imagine the positive and then cancel it out.

50. Avoid buzzwords until such time as you can use them judiciously.

51. I warned them in advance to remove the legalese.

52. I have my own particular way of avoiding vanity in my lucid prose.

53. Make the reader the subject of your sentences throughout the entire sales pitch.

54. Bob is not sure as to whether the mailman is biased.

55. You can avoid bias with the aid of a good style manual.

Even more suggested answers:

36. Ben thinks it's ~~more~~ preferable to put a comma between every pair of elements in a series.

37. All are not averse to the price ~~point~~ of our principal product.

38. The game Line & Link is ~~the one~~ recommended to find mismatches between subject and verb.

39. We will set a ~~new~~ record if all our pronoun references are clear.

40. Writing is not refined ~~in nature~~ if it includes misplaced modifiers.

41. Parallel construction will ~~continue to~~ remain a useful technique.

42. Passive voice and active voice are not ~~one and~~ the same.

43. Passive voice is acceptable in five ~~separate~~ situations.

44. For sentences that are small ~~in size~~, wordiness is seldom a problem.

45. Learn to delete deadwood so that ~~in the future~~ you will not have a problem with wordiness.

46. It is important to understand ~~the fact~~ that bland qualifiers cause imprecise writing.

47. Describe each new ~~type of~~ thing with precise details.

48. ~~In order~~ to avoid negative reactions, don't use words like *avoid*.

49. The ~~most~~ unique thing about negations is that people first imagine the positive and then cancel it out.

50. Avoid buzzwords until ~~such time as~~ you can use them judiciously.

51. I warned them ~~in advance~~ to remove the legalese.

52. I have my own ~~particular~~ way of avoiding vanity in my lucid prose.

53. Make the reader the subject of your sentences throughout the ~~entire~~ sales pitch.

54. Bob is not sure ~~as to~~ whether the mailman is biased.

55. You can avoid bias with ~~the aid of~~ a good style manual.

Redundant Phrases

When we use phrases that are partly redundant, we distract or confuse the reader. Always strive to remove redundancies, such as the words *a time of* in the phrase *a time of two hours* in the following example:

> Ben spent ~~a time of~~ two hours responding to the email.

To practice editing for clarity, learn by guessing: cross out words in redundant phrases and then check your answers on the next page.

1. Following after the reaction to his email, he decided to stop using emoticons.
2. The email generated a total of 28 responses.
3. Most people responded and asked the question, "Why did I get this email?"
4. For the message, Ben assembled together his thoughts about training.
5. With the email, Bob will attach together a spreadsheet.
6. Ben feared the early beginnings of a flame war.
7. However, concern about the email was brief in duration.
8. Administrators told complainers who were replying to Ben's email to cease and desist.
9. A rumor began to circulate around that all emails were being recorded by the security department.
10. Ben's subject line read: Turn the timer in a clockwise direction.
11. If you would collect together my notes, I could combine together my ideas for the letter.
12. The final completion of Bob's letter included an assertive call to action.
13. The consensus of opinion was that ponderous references were inappropriate in a business letter.
14. The first draft of his letter included a weak suggestion to cooperate together.
15. Joint cooperation was requested in the final version.

Suggested answers:

1. Following ~~after~~ the reaction to his email, he decided to stop using emoticons.

2. The email generated ~~a total of~~ 28 responses.

3. Most people responded and asked ~~the question~~, "Why did I get this email?"

4. For the message, Ben assembled ~~together~~ his thoughts about training.

5. With the email, Bob will attach ~~together~~ a spreadsheet.

6. Ben feared the ~~early~~ beginnings of a flame war.

7. However, concern about the email was brief ~~in duration~~.

8. Administrators told complainers who were replying to Ben's email to cease ~~and desist~~.

9. A rumor began to circulate ~~around~~ that all emails were being recorded by the security department.

10. Ben's subject line read: Turn the timer ~~in a~~ clockwise ~~direction~~.

11. If you would collect ~~together~~ my notes, I could combine ~~together~~ my ideas for the letter.

12. The ~~final~~ completion of Bob's letter included an assertive call to action.

13. The consensus ~~of opinion~~ was that ponderous references were inappropriate in a business letter.

14. The first draft of his letter included a weak suggestion to cooperate ~~together~~.

15. ~~Joint~~ cooperation was requested in the final version.

Here are more exercises with redundant phrases:

16. Among the letter recipients we counted eight in number who cooperated.

17. The consensus was that each and every letter was beginning to look like a memo.

18. The resultant effect is that salutations are becoming optional.

19. Enclosed herewith is a memo about ponderous references.

20. A postscript may be included at the final end of the letter.

21. In the ultimate end, the purpose of the resume is to get a job interview.

22. The main essentials of the resume are experience, education, and activities.

23. Use only true facts when listing capabilities and accomplishments.

24. One of the basic fundamentals of writing a resume is to keep it brief.

25. We hope and trust your resume is accurate.

26. In the experience section, list the years of time in each job.

27. No two resumes are exactly identical.

28. His second job was managing foreign imports of electronics.

29. She described the new innovations she introduced as training coordinator.

30. Keywords should be an integral part of a resume submitted online.

31. If we join together the purpose, statements, and ending, we have the core of a memo.

32. If we merge together a new topic with our subject, we risk confusing the reader.

33. Bob wrote that memo at 10:00 AM in the morning.

34. The memo declared our contract to be null and void.

35. In my opinion I think this memo will survive the Embarrassment Test.

More suggested answers:

16. Among the letter recipients we counted eight ~~in number~~ who cooperated.

17. The consensus was that ~~each and~~ every letter was beginning to look like a memo.

18. The ~~resultant~~ effect is that salutations are becoming optional.

19. Enclosed ~~herewith~~ is a memo about ponderous references.

20. A postscript may be included at the ~~final~~ end of the letter.

21. In the ~~ultimate~~ end, the purpose of the resume is to get a job interview.

22. The ~~main~~ essentials of the resume are experience, education, and activities.

23. Use only ~~true~~ facts when listing capabilities and accomplishments.

24. One of the ~~basic~~ fundamentals of writing a resume is to keep it brief.

25. We ~~hope and~~ trust your resume is accurate.

26. In the experience section, list the years ~~of time~~ in each job.

27. No two resumes are ~~exactly~~ identical.

28. His second job was managing ~~foreign~~ imports of electronics.

29. She described the ~~new~~ innovations she introduced as training coordinator.

30. Keywords should be ~~an integral~~ part of a resume submitted online.

31. If we join ~~together~~ the purpose, statements, and ending, we have the core of a memo.

32. If we merge ~~together~~ a new topic with our subject, we risk confusing the reader.

33. Bob wrote that memo at 10:00 AM ~~in the morning~~.

34. The memo declared our contract to be ~~null and~~ void.

35. ~~In my opinion~~ I think this memo will survive the Embarrassment Test.

Here are even more exercises with redundant phrases:

36. Ben's hopeful optimism was evident throughout the memo.

37. During the period from 1998 to 2002 our department archived 400 memos.

38. Archiving the memos requires advance planning for file space.

39. Bob's memo suggested that, at a price of $1000, the computers were a bargain.

40. At the end of the memo, tell readers how you want them to proceed ahead.

41. The report described our forward progress with the pyramid scheme.

42. Adding new sections will prolong the duration of writing the report.

43. All diagrams in the report were rectangular in shape.

44. At the end of the report we will repeat again our conclusions about the budget.

45. To outline with a pyramid, a necessary requisite is the ability to link ideas.

46. The end result is a two-dimensional outline.

47. One of the consequent results is that writing can commence anywhere.

48. Another result is that writing can resume again with ease.

49. Refer back to the last time you had to sit through a long presentation.

50. The headline should be no more that one sentence in length.

51. We drove to the presentation at a rate of 30 miles per hour.

52. The bullet points summarize the present status of the projects.

53. Bob's presentation lasted for a duration of three hours.

54. The honest truth is that the presentation was too long.

55. At the end of the presentation Bob turned in the direction to face the audience.

Even more suggested answers:

36. Ben's ~~hopeful~~ optimism was evident throughout the memo.

37. ~~During the period~~ from 1998 to 2002 our department archived 400 memos.

38. Archiving the memos requires ~~advance~~ planning for file space.

39. Bob's memo suggested that, at ~~a price of~~ $1000, the computers were a bargain.

40. At the end of the memo, tell readers how you want them to proceed ~~ahead~~.

41. The report described our ~~forward~~ progress with the pyramid scheme.

42. Adding new sections will prolong ~~the duration of~~ writing the report.

43. All diagrams in the report were rectangular ~~in shape~~.

44. At the end of the report we will repeat ~~again~~ our conclusions about the budget.

45. To outline with a pyramid, a ~~necessary~~ requisite is the ability to link ideas.

46. The ~~end~~ result is a two-dimensional outline.

47. One of the ~~consequent~~ results is that writing can commence anywhere.

48. Another result is that writing can resume ~~again~~ with ease.

49. Refer ~~back~~ to the last time you had to sit through a long presentation.

50. The headline should be no more that one sentence ~~in length~~.

51. We drove to the presentation at ~~a rate of~~ 30 miles per hour.

52. The bullet points summarize the ~~present~~ status of the projects.

53. Bob's presentation lasted for ~~a duration of~~ three hours.

54. The ~~honest~~ truth is that the presentation was too long.

55. At the end of the presentation Bob turned ~~in the direction~~ to face the audience.

Bureaucratic Verbs

When a verb phrase uses more words than it needs to use but only hints at what it really wants to say, it's acting like a bureaucrat. Here is an example:

> Bob's diagram <u>is an illustration of</u> how to depict a reader.

This sentence speaks with more force and clarity if we unleash the descriptive power of the real verb:

> Bob's diagram **illustrates** how to depict a reader.

In each of the following sentences, locate the bureaucratic verb phrase, cross it out, then suggest a replacement verb.

1. On our Internet connection, peaks in traffic are in excess of 2 Mbps.

2. Next year's budget is dependent on last year's performance.

3. The employees' contention is that the pension fund is in jeopardy.

4. Each section title contains a hint at what comes next.

5. Casual Fridays had an effect on office moral.

6. Bob achieved the establishment of his plans for next year.

7. Ben will accomplish orientation of new hires.

8. Our department manager made a decision to accelerate performance reviews.

9. The sales department makes predictions for increased revenues each quarter.

10. Bob's boss will make reports on our progress.

11. In his presentation he provided a description of the recommended plan of action.

12. Our users' manual makes provisions for simplifying how to use the software.

13. Mr. Smith will give consideration to going to Washington.

14. The negotiation failure occurred because neither side would compromise.

15. Each cubicle is provided with two file cabinets.

Suggested answers:

1. On our Internet connection, peaks in traffic ~~are in excess of~~ 2 Mbps. → **exceed**
2. Next year's budget ~~is dependent on~~ last year's performance. → **depends on**
3. The ~~employees' contention is that~~ the pension fund is in jeopardy. → **employees contend that**
4. Each section title ~~contains a hint at~~ what comes next. → **hints at**
5. Casual Fridays ~~had an effect on~~ office moral. → **affected**
6. Bob ~~achieved the establishment of~~ his plans for next year. → **established**
7. Ben will ~~accomplish orientation of~~ new hires. → **orient**
8. Our department manager ~~made a decision to~~ accelerate performance reviews. → **decided to**
9. The sales department ~~makes predictions for~~ increased revenues each quarter. → **predicts**
10. Bob's boss will ~~make reports on~~ our progress. → **report on**
11. In his presentation he ~~provided a description of~~ the recommended plan of action. → **described**
12. Our users' manual ~~makes provisions for simplifying~~ how to use the software. → **simplifies**
13. Mr. Smith will ~~give consideration to~~ going to Washington. → **consider**
14. The negotiation ~~failure occurred~~ because neither side would compromise. → **failed**
15. Each cubicle ~~is provided with~~ two file cabinets. → **has**

Schizophrenic Verbs

When we use a generic verb that has multiple meanings we leave it up to our readers to decide which sense, or personality, of the verb is the proper one. Here is an example:

> The policy <u>covered</u> new employees for major medical expenses.

The verb *cover* can mean *conceal*, *clothe*, *insure*, *deal with*, or *report details*. Thus, in the reader's mind the word *cover* might conjure up confusing associations with alternate definitions. To avoid this, we can usually substitute a lean verb that says what we really meant:

> The policy **insured** new employees for major medical expenses.

In each of the following sentences, locate the schizophrenic verb phrase, cross it out, then suggest a replacement verb.

1. The new budget represents our biggest problem.
2. By being observant, Bob acquired a better understanding of office politics.
3. Bob and Ben wanted to achieve their best.
4. After the workshop, they employed their new skills to rewrite that proposal.
5. Bob's writing illustrates how to use parallel construction.
6. Using email, Bob supplied a reminder about the upcoming meeting.
7. The email also presents information about prior meetings.
8. The meeting is likely to terminate after the vote on the amendment.
9. We accomplished the survey with great difficulty.
10. After three meetings, we determined that the policy was flawed.
11. All supervisors will soon initiate their performance reviews.
12. In his memo, Ben established that our conclusions were wrong.
13. Bob wonders whether the memo exhibits enough data.
14. Bob and Ben both utilize inexpensive pencils.
15. Please describe the speech you will perform at the offsite meeting.

Your answers may be different but appropriate. It depends on how you interpreted each sentence.

Suggested answers:

1. The new budget ~~represents~~ our biggest problem. → **is**
2. By being observant, Bob ~~acquired~~ a better understanding of office politics. → **gained**
3. Bob and Ben wanted to ~~achieve~~ their best. → **do**
4. After the workshop, they ~~employed~~ their new skills to rewrite that proposal. → **used**
5. Bob's writing ~~illustrates~~ how to use parallel construction. → **shows**
6. Using email, Bob ~~supplied~~ a reminder about the upcoming meeting. → **sent**
7. The email also ~~presents~~ information about prior meetings. → **gives**
8. The meeting is likely to ~~terminate~~ after the vote on the amendment. → **end**
9. We ~~accomplished~~ the survey with great difficulty. → **finished**
10. After three meetings, we ~~determined~~ that the policy was flawed. → **concluded**
11. All supervisors will soon ~~initiate~~ their performance reviews. → **start**
12. In his memo, Ben ~~established~~ that our conclusions were wrong. → **proved**
13. Bob wonders whether the memo ~~exhibits~~ enough data. → **has**
14. Bob and Ben both ~~utilize~~ inexpensive pencils. → **use**
15. Please describe the speech you will ~~perform~~ at the offsite meeting. → **make**

PRACTICE WITH IDIOM

The proper way to say something in English is often a matter of custom. Accepted usage dictates that it be said a certain way. This is idiom. There are three main types of idiom: phrases, prepositions, and grammar. There are thousands of idiomatic phrases. Consult a good dictionary if you are unsure whether a phrase is idiomatic. To find it, look up the most significant word in the phrase: it's usually a verb. In this workbook we concentrate on idiomatic prepositions and grammar, focusing on those that people most often get wrong. We will learn by guessing and then checking our answers on the next page.

Read the following sentences and select the best version:

1 A ☐ According to the plan, the next project should start now.

B ☐ According with the plan, the next project should start now.

2 A ☐ Bob should apologize about the broadcast email.

B ☐ Bob should apologize for the broadcast email.

3 A ☐ It was logical to associate the new contract award and our improved proposals.

B ☐ It was logical to associate the new contract award with our improved proposals.

4 A ☐ Bob and Ben attribute their success to their new writing skills.

B ☐ Bob and Ben attribute their success as being from their new writing skills.

5 A ☐ Ben's decision to start was based on his view that Bob would be late.

B ☐ Ben's decision to start was based around his view that Bob would be late.

6 A ☐ Arguments about bonuses arose between colleagues and among factions.

B ☐ Arguments about bonuses arose among colleagues and between factions.

7 A ☐ Messages traveled back and forth between the personnel office and the sales office.

B ☐ Messages traveled back and forth between the personnel office to the sales office.

8 A ☐ Employees were bored with the cafeteria food.

B ☐ Employees were bored of the cafeteria food.

9 A ☐ The awards were given to both Ben and Bob.

B ☐ The awards were given to both Ben as well as Bob.

1 A ✓ **According to** the plan, the next project should start now.

According with the plan, the next project should start now.

→ **according to X**

2 Bob should apologize about the broadcast email.

B ✓ Bob should **apologize for** the broadcast email.

→ **apologize for X**

3 It was logical to associate the new contract award and our improved proposals.

B ✓ It was logical to **associate** the new contract award **with** our improved proposals.

→ **associate X with Y**

4 A ✓ Bob and Ben **attribute** their success **to** their new writing skills.

Bob and Ben attribute their success as being from their new writing skills.

→ **attribute X to Y**

5 A ✓ Ben's decision to start was **based on** his view that Bob would be late.

Ben's decision to start was based around his view that Bob would be late.

→ **based on X**

6 Arguments about bonuses arose between colleagues and among factions.

B ✓ Arguments about bonuses arose **among colleagues** and **between factions**.

→ **among colleagues** **between factions**

7 A ✓ Messages traveled back and forth **between** the personnel office **and** the sales office.

Messages traveled back and forth between the personnel office to the sales office.

→ **between X and Y**

8 A ✓ Employees were **bored with** the cafeteria food.

Employees were bored of the cafeteria food.

→ **bored with X**

9 A ✓ The awards were given to **both** Ben **and** Bob.

The awards were given to both Ben as well as Bob.

→ **both X and Y**

10 A ☐ To describe differences, Bob compared a memo to a briefing.

B ☐ To describe differences, Bob compared a memo with a briefing.

11 A ☐ To show similarities, Ben compared an email to a letter.

B ☐ To show similarities, Ben compared an email with a letter.

12 A ☐ We were surprised that the CFO complied to the rules.

B ☐ We were surprised that the CFO complied with the rules.

13 A ☐ If we work too hard we may die from exhaustion.

B ☐ If we work too hard we may die of exhaustion.

14 A ☐ Most stories depict Ben to be a voice of reason.

B ☐ Most stories depict Ben as a voice of reason.

15 A ☐ Bob was disappointed at the selection of markers.

B ☐ Bob was disappointed with the selection of markers.

16 A ☐ Ben is able to distinguish inkjet from laser.

B ☐ Ben is able to distinguish inkjet and laser.

17 A ☐ No one expected that the printers would be working.

B ☐ No one expected the printers were working.

C ☐ No one expected the printers to be working.

18 A ☐ In accordance to policy, all projects should start on time.

B ☐ In accordance with policy, all projects should start on time.

10 To describe differences, Bob compared a memo to a briefing.

B ✓ To describe differences, Bob **compared** a memo **with** a briefing.

→ **compared X with Y** (when focused on differences)

11 A ✓ To show similarities, Ben **compared** an email **to** a letter.

To show similarities, Ben compared an email with a letter.

→ **compared X to Y** (when focused on similarities)

12 We were surprised that the CFO complied to the rules.

B ✓ We were surprised that the CFO **complied with** the rules.

→ **complied with X**

13 If we work too hard we may die from exhaustion.

B ✓ If we work too hard we may **die of** exhaustion.

→ **die of exhaustion**

14 Most stories depict Ben to be a voice of reason.

B ✓ Most stories **depict** Ben **as** a voice of reason.

→ **depict X as Y**

15 Bob was disappointed at the selection of markers.

B ✓ Bob was **disappointed with** the selection of markers.

→ **disappointed with X**

16 A ✓ Ben is able to **distinguish** inkjet **from** laser.

Ben is able to distinguish inkjet and laser.

→ **distinguish X from Y**

17 A ✓ No one **expected that** the printers **would be** working.

No one expected the printers were working.

C ✓ No one **expected** the printers **to be** working.

→ **expected that X would be Y** **expected X to be Y**

18 In accordance to policy, all projects should start on time.

B ✓ **In accordance with** policy, all projects should start on time.

→ **in accordance with X**

19 A ☐ Ben's response was delivered independent of Bob's.

B ☐ Ben's response was delivered independent from Bob's.

20 A ☐ Bob went in search for a staple remover.

B ☐ Bob went in search of a staple remover.

21 A ☐ Ben intends to do his exercises while on break.

B ☐ Ben intends on doing his exercises while on break.

22 A ☐ Almost every employee was interested about the new health plans.

B ☐ Almost every employee was interested in the new health plans.

23 A ☐ Bob's report is modeled after Ben's detailed memo.

B ☐ Bob's report is modeled on Ben's detailed memo.

23 A ☐ Ben made no attempt to edit Bob's emails, letters, or memos.

B ☐ Ben made no attempt to edit Bob's emails, letters, nor memos.

25 A ☐ The briefing is not only 40 pages long but also 10 times as boring.

B ☐ The briefing is not only 40 pages long but 10 times as boring.

26 A ☐ Improved performance was caused not so much by raises but instead by praises.

B ☐ Improved performance was caused not so much by raises as by praises.

27 A ☐ It was not the coffee but the pastry that appealed to Ben.

B ☐ It was not the coffee but instead the pastry that appealed to Ben.

19 A ✓ Ben's response was delivered **independent of** Bob's.

Ben's response was delivered <u>independent from</u> Bob's.

→ **independent of X**

20 Bob went <u>in search for</u> a staple remover.

B ✓ Bob went **in search of** a staple remover.

→ **in search of X**

21 A ✓ Ben **intends to do** his exercises while on break.

Ben <u>intends on doing</u> his exercises while on break.

→ **intends to do X**

22 Almost every employee was <u>interested about</u> the new health plans.

B ✓ Almost every employee was **interested in** the new health plans.

→ **interested in X**

23 Bob's report is <u>modeled after</u> Ben's detailed memo.

B ✓ Bob's report is **modeled on** Ben's detailed memo.

→ **modeled on X**

24 A ✓ Ben made **no attempt to** edit Bob's emails, letters, **or** memos.

Ben made <u>no attempt to</u> edit Bob's emails, letters, <u>nor</u> memos.

→ **no attempt to X, Y, or Z**

25 A ✓ The briefing is **not only** 40 pages long **but also** 10 times as boring.

The briefing is <u>not only</u> 40 pages long <u>but</u> 10 times as boring.

→ **not only X but also Y**

26 Improved performance was caused <u>not so much by</u> raises <u>but instead by</u> praises.

B ✓ Improved performance was caused **not so much by** raises **as by** praises.

→ **not so much by X as by Y**

27 A ✓ It was **not the** coffee **but the** pastry that appealed to Ben.

It was <u>not the</u> coffee <u>but instead the</u> pastry that appealed to Ben.

→ **not the X but the Y**

28 A ☐ Does Bob plan to visit the head office?

B ☐ Does Bob plan on visiting the head office?

29 A ☐ Bob and Ben regard the new policies to be winds of change.

B ☐ Bob and Ben regard the new policies as winds of change.

30 A ☐ The result of constructing new cubicles was more privacy.

B ☐ The result from constructing new cubicles was more privacy.

31 A ☐ The new health plan is similar to the old one.

B ☐ The new health plan is similar with the old one.

32 A ☐ The email was so critical it caused everyone to get upset.

B ☐ The email was so critical that it caused everyone to get upset.

33 A ☐ To theorize about office culture is applying management science.

B ☐ To theorize about office culture is to apply management science.

34 A ☐ We will try to see if Ben is finished.

B ☐ We will try and see if Ben is finished.

35 A ☐ Bob was noted for tying the spike in spam with the failure of the firewall.

B ☐ Bob was noted for tying the spike in spam to the failure of the firewall.

36 A ☐ Ben is not worried about the details of the plan.

B ☐ Ben is not worried over the details of the plan.

28 A ✓ Does Bob **plan to** visit the head office?

Does Bob plan on visiting the head office?

→ **plan to X**

29 Bob and Ben regard the new policies to be winds of change.

B ✓ Bob and Ben **regard** the new policies **as** winds of change.

→ **regard X as Y**

30 A ✓ The **result of** constructing new cubicles was more privacy.

The result from constructing new cubicles was more privacy.

→ **result of X**

31 A ✓ The new health plan is **similar to** the old one.

The new health plan is similar with the old one.

→ **similar to X**

32 The email was so critical it caused everyone to get upset.

B ✓ The email was **so** critical **that it** caused everyone to get upset.

→ **so X that it Y**

33 To theorize about office culture is applying management science.

B ✓ **To** theorize about office culture **is to** apply management science.

→ **to X is to Y**

34 A ✓ We will **try to see** if Ben is finished.

We will try and see if Ben is finished.

→ **try to see**

35 Bob was noted for tying the spike in spam with the failure of the firewall.

B ✓ Bob was noted for **tying** the spike in spam **to** the failure of the firewall.

→ **tying X to Y**

36 A ✓ Ben is not **worried about** the details of the plan.

Ben is not worried over the details of the plan.

→ **worried about X**

PRACTICE WITH WORDS

Have you heard the expression *word power is earning power*? It may not be fair, but it is partly true. Your vocabulary determines several things. First, it determines how much you understand in the writing of others at work. Second, it determines how exact or specific you can be with your writing. Third, it determines, at least in part, how others judge your intelligence or level of education. You should view learning (and relearning) useful words as a life-long endeavor. This will be easiest if you can find a way to make such daily learning a fun activity.

One way to expand your vocabulary is to take word quizzes. Here we provide an opportunity for you to expand your business vocabulary with quizzes that feature 100 difficult words that are likely to show up at work. Have fun: learn by guessing and then checking your answers on the next page.

1. A synonym for acquiesce is: demur .. consent .. repose
2. A synonym for ambivalent is: equivocal .. dexterous .. striding
3. A synonym for assiduous is: busy .. rude .. tart
4. A synonym for bolster is: sag .. drink .. support
5. A synonym for celerity is: humor .. haste .. honesty
6. A synonym for coalesce is: join .. clear .. calcify
7. A synonym for concomitant is: numb .. promissory .. associate
8. A synonym for corroborate is: filch .. confirm .. empty
9. A synonym for culpable is: tasty .. blameworthy .. defenseless
10. A synonym for dearth is: ending .. filth .. lack
11. A synonym for discriminate is: distinguish .. deride .. reject
12. A synonym for dissolution is: mixing .. disintegration .. disenchanting
13. A synonym for effectual is: effective .. tender .. terminal
14. A synonym for enigma is: misunderstanding .. mystery .. outcast
15. A synonym for equanimity is: meanness .. popularity .. composure
16. A synonym for exacerbate is: embitter .. appease .. tire
17. A synonym for extant is: alive .. old .. ruined
18. A synonym for extricate is: liberate .. conjecture .. boycott
19. A synonym for hyperbole is: curve .. speech .. exaggeration
20. A synonym for indefatigable is: unforgivable .. tireless .. growing

1. A synonym for acquiesce is: demur .. **consent** .. repose
   acquiesce - to quietly agree without enthusiasm
2. A synonym for ambivalent is: **equivocal** .. dexterous .. striding
   ambivalent - having uncertain or conflicting feelings
3. A synonym for assiduous is: **busy** .. rude .. tart
   assiduous - done persistently with careful attention
4. A synonym for bolster is: sag .. drink .. **support**
   bolster - to prop up or reinforce
5. A synonym for celerity is: humor .. **haste** .. honesty
   celerity - swiftness in moving or acting
6. A synonym for coalesce is: **join** .. clear .. calcify
   coalesce - to unite or grow together into one thing
7. A synonym for concomitant is: numb .. promissory .. **associate**
   concomitant - an accompanying circumstance
8. A synonym for corroborate is: filch .. **confirm** .. empty
   corroborate - to make more certain
9. A synonym for culpable is: tasty .. **blameworthy** .. defenseless
   culpable - deserving blame or censure
10. A synonym for dearth is: ending .. filth .. **lack**
    dearth - an inadequate supply; scarcity of food
11. A synonym for discriminate is: **distinguish** .. deride .. reject
    discriminate - to identify differences
12. A synonym for dissolution is: mixing .. **disintegration** .. disenchanting
    dissolution - the breaking up or ending of something
13. A synonym for effectual is: **effective** .. tender .. terminal
    effectual - valid; able to produce the desired effect
14. A synonym for enigma is: misunderstanding .. **mystery** .. outcast
    enigma - something that baffles or perplexes
15. A synonym for equanimity is: meanness .. popularity .. **composure**
    equanimity - having a disposition not easily disturbed
16. A synonym for exacerbate is: **embitter** .. appease .. tire
    exacerbate - to make more bitter or severe
17. A synonym for extant is: **alive** .. old .. ruined
    extant - still existing; not lost
18. A synonym for extricate is: **liberate** .. conjecture .. boycott
    extricate - to free or disentangle
19. A synonym for hyperbole is: curve .. speech .. **exaggeration**
    hyperbole - a non-literal, exaggerated statement
20. A synonym for indefatigable is: unforgivable .. **tireless** .. growing
    indefatigable - capable of prolonged effort without tiring

21. A synonym for innocuous is: protective .. clumsy .. harmless

22. A synonym for laconic is: obtuse .. profound .. concise

23. A synonym for manifest is: evident .. delicious .. fraternal

24. A synonym for mitigate is: compete .. question .. relieve

25. A synonym for mutable is: quiet .. changeable .. likable

26. A synonym for obfuscate is: obscure .. smooth .. admit

27. A synonym for palpable is: friendly .. unprotected .. evident

28. A synonym for paucity is: stoutness .. tartness .. scarcity

29. A synonym for perfunctory is: penalizing .. automatic .. refusing

30. A synonym for pivotal is: moving .. dangerous .. crucial

31. A synonym for poignant is: indicative .. damaging .. moving

32. A synonym for preclude is: prevent .. predict .. presume

33. A synonym for probity is: integrity .. intelligence .. diligence

34. A synonym for quandary is: protest .. depression .. dilemma

35. A synonym for recondite is: invasive .. abstruse .. amenable

36. A synonym for relegate is: commit .. protest .. aggravate

37. A synonym for resolute is: petulant .. declaring .. unwavering

38. A synonym for rhetoric is: oratory .. hassle .. narrative

39. A synonym for sanction is: scuttle .. investigate .. endorse

40. A synonym for scrutinize is: construct .. examine .. impale

21. A synonym for innocuous is: protective .. clumsy .. **harmless**
innocuous - not harmful; inoffensive or uninteresting

22. A synonym for laconic is: obtuse .. profound .. **concise**
laconic - using few words to express much

23. A synonym for manifest is: **evident** .. delicious .. fraternal
manifest - clearly apparent or obvious

24. A synonym for mitigate is: compete .. question .. **relieve**
mitigate - to make less severe

25. A synonym for mutable is: quiet .. **changeable** .. likable
mutable - able or likely to change

26. A synonym for obfuscate is: **obscure** .. smooth .. admit
obfuscate - to cloud over, or to make unclear

27. A synonym for palpable is: friendly .. unprotected .. **evident**
palpable - capable of being felt

28. A synonym for paucity is: stoutness .. tartness .. **scarcity**
paucity - small number, or insufficient amount

29. A synonym for perfunctory is: penalizing.. **automatic** .. refusing
perfunctory - done routinely with little interest

30. A synonym for pivotal is: moving .. dangerous .. **crucial**
pivotal - of critical importance

31. A synonym for poignant is: indicative .. damaging .. **moving**
poignant - strongly affecting the emotions or senses

32. A synonym for preclude is: **prevent** .. predict .. presume
preclude - to make impossible

33. A synonym for probity is: **integrity** .. intelligence .. diligence
probity - being morally upright

34. A synonym for quandary is: protest .. depression .. **dilemma**
quandary - a state of uncertainty

35. A synonym for recondite is: invasive .. **abstruse** .. amenable
recondite - beyond ordinary understanding

36. A synonym for relegate is: **commit** .. protest .. aggravate
relegate - to consign to an inferior position

37. A synonym for resolute is: petulant .. declaring .. **unwavering**
resolute - showing a firm purpose

38. A synonym for rhetoric is: **oratory** .. hassle .. narrative
rhetoric - effective or showy language

39. A synonym for sanction is: scuttle .. investigate .. **endorse**
sanction - a coercive denial, or to approve

40. A synonym for scrutinize is: construct.. **examine** .. impale
scrutinize - to inspect or observe very carefully

41. A synonym for specious is: rude .. false .. glib
42. A synonym for stalwart is: strong .. handicapped .. homely
43. A synonym for stymie is: dispose .. misbehave .. thwart
44. A synonym for surfeit is: politeness .. need .. excess
45. A synonym for synopsis is: abstract .. connection .. critique
46. A synonym for tepid is: petulant .. dopey .. lukewarm
47. A synonym for trepidation is: awkwardness.. fright .. restraint
48. A synonym for vacillate is: lubricate .. demonstrate .. hesitate
49. A synonym for verisimilitude is: hunger .. plausibility .. lie
50. A synonym for zenith is: apex .. antique .. antihero

Now, to keep things interesting, let's try doing antonyms:

1. An antonym for acclimate is: remain unchanged .. move into .. quietly mock
2. An antonym for adherent is: champion .. renegade .. believer
3. An antonym for apocryphal is: accurate .. spurious .. benign
4. An antonym for auspicious is: propitious .. ominous .. veracious
5. An antonym for capitulate is: submit .. live .. resist
6. An antonym for circumspection is: fastening .. avoidance .. heedlessness
7. An antonym for conciliatory is: antagonizing .. calm .. political
8. An antonym for confound is: discriminate .. praise .. lose
9. An antonym for credulity is: skepticism .. resourcefulness .. confidence
10. An antonym for daunt is: accept .. hearten .. bother

41. A synonym for specious is: rude .. **false** .. glib
specious - appearing correct but lacking merit

42. A synonym for stalwart is: **strong** .. handicapped .. homely
stalwart - very strong and vigorous

43. A synonym for stymie is: dispose .. misbehave .. **thwart**
stymie - to hinder by obstructing

44. A synonym for surfeit is: politeness .. need .. **excess**
surfeit - having or indulging too much

45. A synonym for synopsis is: **abstract** .. connection .. critique
synopsis - a brief overview or summary

46. A synonym for tepid is: petulant .. dopey .. **lukewarm**
tepid - lacking enthusiasm, or moderately warm

47. A synonym for trepidation is: awkwardness .. **fright** .. restraint
trepidation - fearful anxiety, or quivering movement

48. A synonym for vacillate is: lubricate .. demonstrate .. **hesitate**
vacillate - to fluctuate, or to show indecision

49. A synonym for verisimilitude is: hunger .. **plausibility** .. lie
verisimilitude - the quality of seeming to be real or true

50. A synonym for zenith is: **apex** .. antique .. antihero
zenith - the highest or culminating point

1. An antonym for acclimate is: **remain unchanged** .. move into .. quietly mock
acclimate - to accustom oneself to a new environment

2. An antonym for adherent is: champion .. **renegade** .. believer
adherent - someone who supports a leader or cause

3. An antonym for apocryphal is: **accurate** .. spurious .. benign
apocryphal - of doubtful authenticity; counterfeit

4. An antonym for auspicious is: propitious .. **ominous** .. veracious
auspicious - indicating a good future

5. An antonym for capitulate is: submit .. live .. **resist**
capitulate - to surrender with conditions

6. An antonym for circumspection is: fastening .. avoidance .. **heedlessness**
circumspection - considering all consequences before acting

7. An antonym for conciliatory is: **antagonizing** .. calm .. political
conciliatory - tending to win over or soothe

8. An antonym for confound is: **discriminate** .. praise .. lose
confound - to perplex; mistake one thing for another

9. An antonym for credulity is: **skepticism** .. resourcefulness .. confidence
credulity - the tendency to believe with little proof

10. An antonym for daunt is: accept .. **hearten** .. bother
daunt - to scare, or to discourage

11. An antonym for deleterious is: salutary .. detrimental .. bombastic

12. An antonym for dispassionate is: fervent .. unruffled .. wan

13. An antonym for dogmatic is: eager .. quiet .. receptive

14. An antonym for elucidate is: prove .. confuse .. grasp

15. An antonym for entreat is: penalize for .. speed up .. hint at

16. An antonym for espouse is: forsake .. disconnect .. know

17. An antonym for exonerate is: absolve .. welcome .. blame

18. An antonym for extemporaneous is: early .. gentle .. rehearsed

19. An antonym for fortuitous is: deliberate .. fortunate .. unnecessary

20. An antonym for impromptu is: prepared .. premature .. proper

21. An antonym for innate is: legitimate .. single .. acquired

22. An antonym for intrinsic is: enduring .. foreign .. mobile

23. An antonym for lucid is: metallic .. bumpy .. murky

24. An antonym for meticulous is: serious .. sloppy .. calm

25. An antonym for modicum is: iota .. deluge .. constancy

26. An antonym for neophyte is: tyro .. veteran .. serum

27. An antonym for opaque is: transparent .. cheerful .. slippery

28. An antonym for paradigm is: paragon .. exception .. abbreviation

29. An antonym for pedantic is: nonacademic .. nonessential .. nonpartisan

30. An antonym for pithy is: strong .. old .. rambling

11. An antonym for deleterious is: **salutary** .. detrimental .. bombastic
deleterious - injurious to health

12. An antonym for dispassionate is: **fervent** .. unruffled .. wan
dispassionate - unaffected by emotions or bias

13. An antonym for dogmatic is: eager .. quiet .. **receptive**
dogmatic - arrogantly asserting opinions

14. An antonym for elucidate is: prove .. **confuse** .. grasp
elucidate - to make clear

15. An antonym for entreat is: penalize for .. speed up .. **hint at**
entreat - to earnestly request; to ask urgently

16. An antonym for espouse is: **forsake** .. disconnect .. know
espouse - to support or advocate

17. An antonym for exonerate is: absolve .. welcome .. **blame**
exonerate - to free from blame

18. An antonym for extemporaneous is: early .. gentle .. **rehearsed**
extemporaneous - done without special preparation

19. An antonym for fortuitous is: **deliberate** .. fortunate .. unnecessary
fortuitous - happening by chance; bringing good luck

20. An antonym for impromptu is: **prepared** .. premature .. proper
impromptu - done without prior preparation

21. An antonym for innate is: legitimate .. single .. **acquired**
innate - existing in a person as a natural part

22. An antonym for intrinsic is: enduring .. **foreign** .. mobile
intrinsic - belonging to the nature of something

23. An antonym for lucid is: metallic .. bumpy .. **murky**
lucid - bright or easily understood

24. An antonym for meticulous is: serious .. **sloppy** .. calm
meticulous - very careful or concerned with details

25. An antonym for modicum is: iota .. **deluge** .. constancy
modicum - a small quantity

26. An antonym for neophyte is: tyro .. **veteran** .. serum
neophyte - a new convert, or a novice

27. An antonym for opaque is: **transparent** .. cheerful .. slippery
opaque - not allowing light to pass through

28. An antonym for paradigm is: paragon .. **exception** .. abbreviation
paradigm - example conjugation, or a model

29. An antonym for pedantic is: **nonacademic** .. nonessential .. nonpartisan
pedantic - overemphasizing trivial points of learning

30. An antonym for pithy is: strong .. old .. **rambling**
pithy - brief but full of meaning

31. An antonym for plethora is: surfeit .. discord .. dearth

32. An antonym for precarious is: safe .. robust .. ambitious

33. An antonym for prevaricate is: confront .. equivocate .. ignore

34. An antonym for propensity is: loyalty .. aversion .. anticipate

35. An antonym for quiescent is: active .. latent .. obvious

36. An antonym for regimen is: fixed plan .. slow retreat .. lax activity

37. An antonym for repudiate is: disown .. approve .. assemble

38. An antonym for reticent is: excited .. talkative .. moving

39. An antonym for salutation is: orchestration .. reputation .. valediction

40. An antonym for scrupulous is: remiss .. exacting .. munificent

41. An antonym for solicit is: refuse to spend .. not listen .. avoid seeking

42. An antonym for spurious is: boring .. restraining .. authentic

43. An antonym for stratagem is: candid plan .. sly contrivance .. quick design

44. An antonym for superfluous is: unnecessary .. pleasing .. deficient

45. An antonym for surmise is: insult .. creation .. certainty

46. An antonym for tacit is: frenzied .. unrestricted .. voiced

47. An antonym for terse is: appreciative .. wise .. repetitious

48. An antonym for trite is: stock .. original .. prolonged

49. An antonym for verbose is: kind .. satisfied .. terse

50. An antonym for volition is: coercion .. election .. quietude

31. An antonym for plethora is: surfeit .. discord .. **dearth**
plethora - an excess or overabundance

32. An antonym for precarious is: **safe** .. robust .. ambitious
precarious - perilous, or dependent on uncertainties

33. An antonym for prevaricate is: **confront** .. equivocate .. ignore
prevaricate - to speak evading the truth

34. An antonym for propensity is: loyalty .. **aversion** .. anticipate
propensity - a natural tendency or bent

35. An antonym for quiescent is: **active** .. latent .. obvious
quiescent - resting, or being quiet and still

36. An antonym for regimen is: fixed plan .. slow retreat .. **lax activity**
regimen - a regulated course of action

37. An antonym for repudiate is: disown .. **approve** .. assemble
repudiate - to publicly reject or disclaim

38. An antonym for reticent is: excited .. **talkative** .. moving
reticent - disinclined to speak readily

39. An antonym for salutation is: orchestration .. reputation .. **valediction**
salutation - an expression of greeting or good will

40. An antonym for scrupulous is: **remiss** .. exacting .. munificent
scrupulous - conscientiously honest; demanding

41. An antonym for solicit is: refuse to spend .. not listen .. **avoid seeking**
solicit - to ask earnestly, or to tempt

42. An antonym for spurious is: boring .. restraining .. **authentic**
spurious - fake, or not genuine

43. An antonym for stratagem is: **candid plan** .. sly contrivance .. quick design
stratagem - a scheme of deception

44. An antonym for superfluous is: unnecessary .. pleasing .. **deficient**
superfluous - exceeding what is necessary

45. An antonym for surmise is: insult .. creation .. **certainty**
surmise - a guess, or to infer without evidence

46. An antonym for tacit is: frenzied .. unrestricted .. **voiced**
tacit - being silent; understood without saying

47. An antonym for terse is: appreciative .. wise .. **repetitious**
terse - brief but often elegant

48. An antonym for trite is: stock .. **original** .. prolonged
trite - lacking appeal because of overuse

49. An antonym for verbose is: kind .. satisfied .. **terse**
verbose - using more words than needed

50. An antonym for volition is: **coercion** .. election .. quietude
volition - the act of using the will